D1360766

CYBERSAFETY

St. Mary's High School

Cyberpredators

CYBERSAFETY

CYBERSAFETY

Cyberpredators

JAMES P. COLT, Ed. D.

CONSULTING EDITOR

MARCUS K. ROGERS, Ph.D., CISSP, DFCP

Founder and Director,
Cyber Forensics Program,
Purdue University

 CHELSEA HOUSE

An Infobase Learning Company

Cybersafety: Cyberpredators

Copyright © 2011 by Infobase Learning

All rights reserved. No part of this book may be reproduced or utilized in any form or by any means, electronic or mechanical, including photocopying, recording, or by any information storage or retrieval systems, without permission in writing from the publisher. For information contact:

Chelsea House
An Infobase Learning Company
132 West 31st Street
New York NY 10001

Library of Congress Cataloging-in-Publication Data
Colt, James P.
  Cyberpredators / James P. Colt. — 1st ed.
     p. cm. — (Cybersafety)
  Includes bibliographical references and index.
  ISBN-13: 978-1-60413-698-2 (hardcover : alk. paper)
  ISBN-10: 1-60413-698-7 (hardcover : alk. paper) 1. Computer crimes—Juvenile literature.
2. World Wide Web—Security measures—Juvenile literature. 3. Internet—Security measures—Juvenile literature. I. Title. II. Series.

  HV6773.C648 2011
  005.8—dc22   2010044345

Chelsea House books are available at special discounts when purchased in bulk quantities for businesses, associations, institutions, or sales promotions. Please call our Special Sales Department in New York at (212) 967-8800 or (800) 322-8755.

You can find Chelsea House on the World Wide Web at http://www.infobasepublishing.com

Text design by Erik Lindstrom
Cover design by Takeshi Takahashi
Composition by EJB Publishing Services
Cover printed by Yurchak Printing, Landisville, Pa.
Book printed and bound by Yurchak Printing, Landisville, Pa.
Date printed: May 2011

Printed in the United States of America

10 9 8 7 6 5 4 3 2 1

This book is printed on acid-free paper.

All links and Web addresses were checked and verified to be correct at the time of publication. Because of the dynamic nature of the Web, some addresses and links may have changed since publication and may no longer be valid.

CONTENTS

Foreword

The Internet has had and will continue to have a profound effect on society. It is hard to imagine life without such technologies as computers, cell phones, gaming devices, and so on. The Internet, World Wide Web, and their associated technologies have altered our social and personal experience of the world. In no other time in history have we had such access to knowledge and raw information. One can search the Library of Congress, the Louvre in Paris, and read online books and articles or watch videos from just about any country in the world. We can interact and chat with friends down the street, in another state, or half way around the globe. The world is now our neighborhood. We are a "wired" society who lives a significant amount of our life online and tethered to technology.

The Internet, or cyberspace, is a great enabler. What is also becoming apparent, though, is that there is a dark side to this global wired society. As the concept of who our friends are moves from real world relationships to cyberspace connections, so also do the rules change regarding social conventions and norms. How many friends do we have online that we have actually met in person? Are online-only friends even real or at the very least whom they claim to be? We also begin to redefine privacy. Questions arise over what should be considered private or public information. Do we really want everyone in the global society to have access to our personal information? As with the real world there may be people online that we do not wish to associate with or grant access to our lives.

It is easy to become enamored with technology and the technology/information revolution. It is equally as easy to become paranoid about the dangers inherent in cyberspace. What is difficult but necessary is to be realistic about how our world has been forever changed. We see numerous magazine, TV, and newspaper headlines regarding the latest cybercrime attacks. Stories about identity theft being the fastest growing non-violent criminal activity are common. The government is concerned with cyber or information warfare attacks against critical infrastructures. Given this kind of media coverage it is easy to think that the sky is falling and cyberspace is somehow evil. Yet if we step back and think about it, technology is neither good nor bad, it simply *is*. Technology is neutral; it is what we do with technology that determines whether it improves our lives or damages and makes our lives more difficult. Even if someone is on the proverbial fence over whether the Internet and cyberspace are society enablers or disablers, what is certain is that the technology genie is out of the bottle. We will never be able to put it back in; we need to learn how to master and live with it.

Learning to live with the Internet and its technological offshoots is one of the objectives behind the Cybersafety series of books. The immortal words of Sir Francis Bacon (the father of the scientific method) "knowledge is power" ring especially true today. If we live in a society that is dependent on technology and therefore we live a significant portion of our daily lives in cyberspace, then we need to understand the potential downside as well as the upside. However, what is not useful is fear mongering or the demonization of technology.

There is no doubt that cyberspace has its share of bad actors and criminals. This should not come as a surprise to anyone. Cyberspace mirrors traditional society, including both the good and unfortunately the bad. Historically criminals have been attracted to new technologies in an effort to improve and extend their criminal methods. The same advantages that technology and cyberspace bring to our normal everyday lives (e.g., increased communication, the ability to remotely access information) can be used in a criminal manner. Online fraud, identity theft, cyberstalking, and cyberbullying are but a few of the ugly behaviors that we see online today.

Navigating successfully through cyberspace also means that we need to understand how the "cyber" affects our personality and social behavior. One of the empowering facets of cyberspace and technology is the fact that we can escape reality and find creative outlets for ourselves. We can immerse ourselves in computer and online games, and if so inclined, satisfy our desire to gamble or engage in other risky behaviors. The sense of anonymity and the ability to redefine who we are online can be intoxicating to some people. We can experiment with new roles and behaviors that may be polar opposites of who we are in the real physical world. Yet, as in the real world, our activities and behaviors in cyberspace have consequences too. Well-meaning escapism can turn to online addictions; seemingly harmless distractions like online gaming can consume so much of our time that our real world relationships and lives are negatively affected. The presumed anonymity afforded by cyberspace can lead to bullying and stalking, behaviors that can have a profound and damaging impact on the victims and on ourselves.

The philosophy behind the Cybersafety series is based on the recognition that cyberspace and technology will continue to play an increasingly important part of our everyday lives. The way in which we define who we are, our home life, school, social relationships, and work life will all be influenced and impacted by our online behaviors and misbehaviors. Our historical notions of privacy will also be redefined in terms of universal access to our everyday activities and posted musings. The Cybersafety series was created to assist us in understanding and making sense of the online world. The intended audience for the series is those individuals who are and will be the most directly affected by cyberspace and its technologies, namely young people (i.e., those in grades 6 -12).

Young people are the future of our society. It is they who will go forward and shape societal norms, customs, public policy, draft new laws, and be our leaders. They will be tasked with developing positive coping mechanisms for both the physical and cyberworlds. They will have dual citizenship responsibilities: citizens of the physical and of the cyber. It is hoped that this series will assist in providing insight, guidance, and positive advice for this journey.

The series is divided into books that logically gather related concepts and issues. The goal of each book in the series is not to scare but to educate and inform the reader. As the title of the series states the focus is on "safety." Each book in the series provides advice on what to watch out for and how to be safer. The emphasis is on education and awareness while providing a frank discussion related to the consequences of certain online behaviors.

It is my sincere pleasure and honor to be associated with this series. As a former law enforcement officer and current educator, I am all too aware of the dangers that can befall our young people. I am also keenly aware that young people are more astute than some adults commonly give them credit for being. Therefore it is imperative that we begin a dialogue that enhances our awareness and encourages and challenges the reader to reexamine their behaviors and attitudes toward cyberspace and technology. We fear what we do not understand; fear is not productive, but knowledge is empowering. So let's begin our collective journey into arming ourselves with more knowledge.

—Marcus K. Rogers, Ph. D., CISSP, DFCP,
Founder and Director,
Cyber Forensics Program,
Purdue University

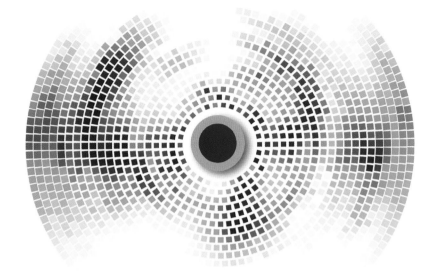

Introduction

Don't talk to strangers! For generations, this message was commonly given to kids by their parents as a reminder to be wary of would-be kidnappers, rapists, and predators. In the age of the Internet, this advice no longer seems to apply. With modern digital communications, avoiding unknown individuals can be difficult. In fact, teenagers and other young people often go online with the *intention* of meeting and talking to strangers. Isn't that what the Internet is all about? The modern and current reality is that young people routinely "friend" and communicate with numerous strangers online. Yet, they rarely think about whom it *really* is that they are talking to, and that an imminent threat to their well-being may be just a mouse-click away. Now, the popular message of not talking to strangers has changed, or *should* change, to how do you *safely* talk with strangers online?

Unfortunately, there is always a chance that the person a teen is talking with online is not who they seem. People have been shown to be less than truthful while in the online world. Many people lie about their age, gender, occupation, and numerous other things. Even worse, the individual on the other end of the Internet connection may be something much darker than a teen could imagine. He or she may be a cyberpredator attempting to groom their young prey or lure them into a violent trap. The risks for many young individuals falling into this trap increase while using the Internet, as young people tend to say and post messages that they would never share in person or in public. While online, young people feel that they are invisible and anonymous, and often do not consider how others may respond to their words or actions. As a result, they are more likely to engage in risky behaviors online, while failing to consider how a cyberpredator operates. The story of Christina Long illustrates this point.

In 2002, 13-year-old Christina Long of Danbury, Connecticut, became the first confirmed victim murdered by a sexual cyberpredator in the United States.[1] Long came from a loving home, and despite some trouble early in her life, she did not seem to fit the profile of a victim. She was a popular honors student and cheerleader while at school. At night while using the Internet, however, she appeared to be a different person altogether. For example, she made it clear through posts to a Web site that she was ready for anything. While online, she also expressed her desire to engage in risky behavior and even appeared to seek out sexual partners. It was on the Internet where she met Saul Dos Reis, a married restaurant worker.

Christina and her aunt, Shelley Riling, were close, and Shelley had explained the possible online dangers to her niece. She even had Christina change her screen name because she thought it was too provocative and advised Christina to change her Web site so that it would look less suggestive. On some Friday evenings, she would drop Christina off at the mall for a few hours, and it was at the mall where Christina met Dos Reis in person, the 25-year-old man who murdered her. According to prosecutors, Dos Reis strangled Long in his vehicle after they had sex at the mall parking lot, and then dumped her body in a shallow stream.

Shelley Riling holds a photograph of her niece, Christina Long, outside the Bridgeport, Connecticut, federal court after the sentencing of Saul Dos Reis. Dos Reis, already serving 30 years on state charges for the death of the 13-year-old girl, was sentenced to an additional 25 years in prison on federal charges. (*AP Photo/Douglas Healey*)

Dos Reis claimed that Long was fascinated with rough sex and that she prompted Dos Reis to choke her while having sex. During the encounter, he claimed that she lost consciousness, and when he realized she was dead, he attempted to do mouth-to-mouth and tasted blood. After panicking and driving her body around for nearly an hour, he then dumped her body in a stream near his home. Dos Reis was sentenced under state law to 30 years in prison for the crimes of manslaughter and sexual assault and another 25 years on federal charges.[2]

The picture that usually comes to mind when hearing the word cyberpredator is that of a scary, wild-eyed sociopath. The even-more frightening truth is that there is no one profile of a cyberpredator. Rather, the cyberpredator can be a teacher, a lawyer, a computer technician, a multimillionaire mortgage broker, a coach, a factory worker, a legislator, a priest, a businessman, or a female-child pornographer. Other than being usually adult males, there is no look, age, profession, or any other characteristic that definitely identifies a person as a cyberpredator. Cyberpredators can be professional or unemployed, educated or uneducated. They can be young or old. They can be convicted criminals with a history of abuse, and they can be others who have never even been pulled over by a police officer, let alone ticketed for speeding.

Though the lack of a profile makes it more difficult for law enforcement to track and catch cyberpredators, there exists a nationwide network through the National Center for Missing and Exploited Children (NCMEC), which operates the CyberTipline to report crimes against children or suspicious behavior. Further, federal and local law enforcement have stepped up efforts to find and remove cyberpredators from both the virtual and real worlds. Still, the problem is too big for law enforcement to handle alone: there are simply not enough cyberpolice to patrol the Internet. In addition, young people are not being educated effectively about the dangers at their fingertips, despite almost limitless opportunities to be exposed to a cyberpredator. But it is never too late to try and catch up, and this book is a start.

Christina Long was found murdered after meeting Saul Dos Reis at the Danbury Fair Mall in Danbury, Connecticut. (NY Daily News *via Getty Images*)

Chapter 1 (What Is a Cyberpredator?) explores the definition of a cyberpredator and what differentiates cyberpredators from other types of online offenders.

Chapter 2 (Young People and Technology) examines the use of technology by young people and the connection between increased use of technology and increased risk of being a victim.

Chapter 3 (The Vulnerability of Being Online) reviews the nature of online communications and why young online users are particularly vulnerable.

Chapter 4 (Using Technology to Ensnare Their Prey) describes the various technological means by which cyberpredators ensnare their prey.

SHOT TO DEATH
BY A CYBERPREDATOR

Amy Boyer was a 20-year-old woman who was described by her mother and stepfather as happy and successful. Everything changed when, in 1999, a cyberpredator stalked and killed her. He waited for her to get into her car and then drove up next to her in his vehicle. He called out her name and put a gun out his window and pressed it against her window. When she looked up, it was over. The shooter, Liam Youens, 21, then shot and killed himself just moments later.[4]

Initially, the case was confusing because there did not appear to be a connection between Youens and Boyer. Boyer's stepfather was shocked that someone could hate so much to do something like this and even more shocked that he had never even heard the shooter's name before. Answers finally started to surface when police searched Youens' computer.

What they found was a Web site that Youens had created titled "Amy Boyer." The site chronicled how Youens had stalked Boyer for years and also described how much he wanted to kill her. In fact, the site described in advance how the murder would take place, which was exactly the same as how it actually happened. The Web site had existed for about two and a half years, but it is unknown as to how many people had seen it.

On the site, Youens described how he had fallen for Boyer in the eighth grade, but that she had rejected him. He decided then that she must die. Boyer probably never thought about Youens again after rejecting him in the eighth grade. She simply did not know him, but he certainly knew her.

Chapter 5 (Characteristics, Types, and Tactics) documents the infamous case of John Robinson, covers the characteristics and tactics of a cyberpredator, and explores the psychology of a cyberpredator. The chapter also details types of cyberpredators, including sexual predators, murderers, stalkers, and others.

Chapter 6 (Laws, Investigations, and Legal Issues) examines the legal issues, criminal and civil laws, and the investigation and prosecution procedures used by law enforcement.

Chapter 7 (Using Knowledge for Protection: Online Self-Defense) offers advice to help young people to defend themselves in a changing, digital world.

Statistics from the Federal Bureau of Investigation indicate that the chances of being violently victimized by a cyberpredator are rare. In fact, young people are much more likely to be a victim of online bullying by one of their peers or "friends." Research has shown that the majority of online offenses involving children are committed by peers that are close in age.[3] Even though being a victim of a violent cyberpredator is rare statistically, however, it *still happens*. And when it does happen, it can be especially heinous and involve sexual abuse, torture, and death. Yet, contrary to this violent image, the most common cyberpredator is the adult sex offender who uses the technology to seduce younger victims. With this in mind, young people need to change their thinking, from "it will never happen to me" to "something really could happen to me so it is important to be careful online." At any given moment across the world, there are cyberpredators communicating *in the rooms of young people*, often with the intent of luring them into a meeting and causing them harm. Cyberpredators are simply too close to ignore.

What Is
a Cyberpredator?

In 2009, 20-year-old Michael John Anderson was convicted of first-degree premeditated murder for the shooting death of 24-year-old Katherine Ann Olson. For this crime, and conviction for other charges, he was sentenced to life in prison without the possibility of parole. What made this different from other homicides? Anderson used technology to help him lure and kill his victim. Specifically, he ran a phony advertisement on the Web site Craigslist, seeking a babysitter. Upon responding to the ad and meeting Anderson in his home, Olson was fatally shot in the back. Anderson then hid Olson's body in the trunk of her car. Anderson's defense attorney argued that he lured Olson to his home with no clear intentions. The defense claimed that when she tried to leave, however, he pulled a gun and accidently shot her after he tripped or flinched. Prosecutors, on the other hand, asserted that Anderson ran the phony online ad to lure her to his home so that he could experience what it felt like to kill.

Unlike an assumption that predators are always older people preying on the young, Anderson was an adult male preying on an older woman in her mid-twenties. Olson was not the only victim in this case. Olson's family, who also had to experience loss and trauma, were also victims. Olson's older sister experienced sleep problems because she could not stop thinking about images from the murder. She was "haunted by Anderson's face, by Katherine's screams, the gun, her body in the trunk and now, the real bloody images of my sister."[1] County Attorney Patrick Ciliberto also had strong words: "As much of a good force that the Internet is, it is also a force for evil." This was the first known case of a Craigslist killer.

Before the emergence of the Internet, sex offenders, pedophiles, and stalkers used a very different modus operandi, or method of operation, to target and attack their victims. Now, rather than searching for victims on the playground or at malls, the modern predator has an immediate and anonymous means to identify, communicate, interact with, and hurt all types of potential victims. According to Merriam-Webster's, a predator is defined as one that preys, destroys, or devours; and predatory means inclined or intended to injure or exploit others for personal gain or profit. Prey, on the other hand, is defined as a victim, one that is defenseless, especially during an attack. A cyberpredator, then, may be defined as one who uses information technology, such as computers, to select victims and to facilitate the attack and victimization of others. Yet, this definition does not seem to capture the more powerful, seductive, deliberate, and dangerous nature of cyberpredators, as compared to other Internet offenders such as hackers and bullies. While the chance of being a victim of a cyberpredator is far less than that of being a victim of cyberbullying or identity theft, the overall threat to individual well-being associated with this type of victimization makes it equally, if not more, relevant than other types of online victimization.

So just how can the term cyberpredator *be defined*? In general terms it would seem that most cybercriminals or cyberoffenders use information technology to facilitate the attack and victimization of others. For example, denial of service (DOS) attacks involve an attempt to deny computer users access to an information system or resources.[2] This may be done by flooding computer networks with

Katherine Ann Olson

September 16, 1983 - October 25, 2007

October 31, 2007
2 p.m.
Christ Presbyterian Church
Edina, Minnesota

*The light shines in the darkness,
and the darkness did not overcome it.*

John 1:5

Katherine Ann Olson was shot and killed after responding to a Craigslist ad seeking a babysitter. (*AP Photo/Jim Mone*) such a large amount of data that servers are unable to keep up with network traffic. The goal of DOS attacks is to prevent or disrupt network traffic. One well-publicized example was the DOS attack on the Web site Twitter, which caused the site to be down for several hours in August of 2009. Other popular Internet sites such as Yahoo, eBay, and Amazon have been targeted, which not only inconvenienced or annoyed computer users, but also caused as much as an estimated $1.7 billion in lost revenue and damages.[3] Yet, despite this disruption and harm, the criminals responsible for DOS attacks do not fit the definition of a cyberpredator.

Similarly, criminals use many other tricks and schemes, usually with the goal of defrauding people and trying to steal their money. These tricks involving online theft are so common now that it is estimated that they equal or surpass the number of traffic violations observed on roads and highways.[4] One example is credit card fraud, which often involves impersonating another individual to gain access to his or her financial accounts and then buying items or services using the other person's name and credit account. Other tricks include identity theft and spoofing, which involves tricking people into giving up personal confidential information (through e-mail or instant message) that can be used to commit crimes. Phishing is another way criminals, either alone or within organized networks, can deceive users into going to Web sites in order to get to their personal information. Phishing involves trying to get people to reveal private information such as bank account numbers. To accomplish this, criminals often pretend that they are a trusted organization such as a bank and persuade potential victims to send their account numbers. Hackers are another type of online offender, who attempt to "break into" or gain unauthorized access to information systems. Again, however, even though these tricks and schemes can be criminal and harmful, they still are not associated with cyberpredators. The same can be said for criminals such as malicious code writers, entertainment pirates, academic cheats, and those who use technology for espionage, or spying. While they may be criminals, they are not really considered cyberpredators.

THE STORY OF EDWARD T. BYRD: THE MULTIMILLIONAIRE CYBERPREDATOR

Cyberpredators do not have a clear profile, which can make it hard for law enforcement to pinpoint them. While they are usually men, these men have many different personality characteristics, occupations, intentions, and methods. They can range from being sadistic serial killers who lure their victims through the Internet, to rich businessmen who seduce their victims. For example, multimillionaire mortgage banker Edward T. Byrd was not only a successful businessman, he was also a cyberpredator. Byrd, the 57-year-old president of Edward T. Byrd & Co., began sending and receiving e-mails with (whom he thought was) a young girl he met in an Internet chat room. He eventually boarded an airplane and flew from Orlando to Oklahoma City to meet with the 13-year-old virgin girl. Byrd's plan was to teach the girl how to have sex "properly and painlessly," but the plan quickly changed when he found out that the "girl" was really an FBI agent. Byrd was taken into custody in the motel lobby where he had planned to meet the child, and faced federal charges. When confronted by federal agents, he reportedly tried to back away, turned white, put his head down, and stated that he was not going to do anything.[10]

Offenders that come closer to the current notion of a cyberpredator are certain cyberbullies and cyberstalkers. For example, cyberbullying involves using information technology to intimidate, harass, annoy, threaten, embarrass, or otherwise cause harm to a targeted individual or group of individuals.[5] Cyberbullying can be done in a number of ways, using a number of different methods involving communications technology. For example, a cyberbully can use e-mail, IM, texts, or Web posts to insult, spread rumors, impersonate, exclude, or threaten others. Although cyberbullying can be very destructive for its victims, it would not be considered a cyberpredator case unless it involved the more serious crime of cyberstalking. One could certainly make the argument that cyber-bullies are also cyberpredators because their behaviors are intentional, repeated, harmful, and involve an imbalance of power.

In cyberstalking and cyberpredator cases, however, the level of the victim's fear, distress, or personal vulnerability is often intensified and therefore considered more severe. This is the key distinction between a cyberpredator, and other types of online offenders: *Cyberpredator cases result in significant personal or emotional harm for individuals who are unable, or incapable, of defending themselves due to age, gender, or other personal vulnerability or circumstances.* Therefore, similar to definitions of bullying, there is often an imbalance of power, with the cyberpredator having more power than their victims. In other words, the cyberpredator has an advantage because they have targeted someone because they are weak or vulnerable in some way. For example, the target may be very young and naïve about forming relationships with others online, or they may be experiencing other personal problems such as being lonely, depressed, or have family issues. This vulnerability is magnified given the nature of online communications and the lack of in-person contact. Online cyberpredators can easily hide their true intentions because their victims cannot see or hear them. Therefore, they have a sense of power because they are able to control and manipulate their victims.

Generally, the most common vulnerability is the age of victims. For example, if adults use technology to prey on children, then those adults are cyberpredators. The children may be young teens and "minors" in the eyes of the law, and these young people sometimes voluntarily agree to meet with predators. Children and young people can be more vulnerable online because they do not have the life experiences or maturity to recognize that they may be dealing with someone who is trying to hurt them. It may be difficult for them to identify a cyberpredator who is trying to manipulate them

(continues on page 26)

WAS LORI DREW A CYBERPREDATOR?

On October 17, 2006, a 13-year-old girl from Missouri, named Megan Meier, committed suicide. While on MySpace, Megan became friends with a boy named "Josh Evans." Josh was initially very kind and complimentary, calling Megan "hot." But this quickly changed, and the kindness turned to cruelty as Josh became extremely insulting. He told Megan that he hated her, and other girls on MySpace piled on with insults of their own. Shortly afterward, Megan (who suffered from depression) hanged herself with a belt. On the day she committed suicide, a hurt and confused Megan sent a message to Josh saying, "I just don't understand why u acttin like this."[8]

The investigation into Megan's death revealed that Josh was actually a fake profile created by a 48-year-old mother of another girl who Megan knew. The mother, Lori Drew, reportedly stated to police that she, along with a female teenager, created the profile of Josh Evans in order to secretly monitor what Megan was saying on MySpace about her daughter. Missouri prosecutors intended to charge Drew with a crime but could not find an appropriate statute. Drew was later charged by federal prosecutors in California under the Computer Fraud and Abuse Act, which is an anti-hacking statute, and was convicted of three misdemeanor charges. A federal judge overturned the guilty verdicts against Drew, however, because of the vague wording of the statute and because he did not agree with the argument that violating the terms of service of MySpace constituted computer hacking. While some legislation has been proposed following the case that called for either more severe punishments or more education, the case showed that it can be difficult to apply the law to certain cases of cyberharassment.

Despite the legal ruling, was Lori Drew a cyberpredator? An adult woman using technology to impersonate a boy in order to manipulate a young girl seems to indicate a power difference in favor of Drew. Perhaps more significant, Meier was extremely vulnerable due to age, mental health, and personal circumstances. Drew appeared to exploit this vulnerability and cause severe emotional harm. Some may argue that Drew was not a cyberpredator because she did not intend to have Meier kill herself. Another argument can be made, however, that although this is a different kind of incident, Drew was still a cyberpredator given the fact that she was an adult who used technology to prey upon a young girl and inflict emotional harm. Still, Drew consistently argued that it was not her idea to create the account and fake profile, but she was involved nonetheless. The final messages to Meier actually came from Ashley Grills, an 18-year-old friend of the Drews, who admitted to sending to Meier, "You are a bad person and everybody hates you. The world would be a better place without you."

Lori Drew, a Missouri woman who perpetrated a MySpace hoax that drove 13-year-old Megan Meier to suicide, leaves court with her attorney. *(AP Photo/ Nick Ut)*

(continued from page 23)

through deceit over a period of time. On the other hand, a predator is sometimes honest about their intentions with their victims, but very young victims may not realize that forming a relationship with them is wrong. Either way, predators are still intentionally forming an online relationship with a young person in order to exploit them later. The exploitation often results in a level of harm that is often psychological, similar to molestation. Yet, simply put, online predation can also be more destructive, dangerous, and violent than other types of online offenses.

Cyberpredators such as violent stalkers, murderers, and those who target the young are responsible for causing physical harm, sexual abuse, or even death to their victims. Although being a victim of a cyberpredator is much less likely than being a victim of cyberbullying or identity theft, it is more likely that these victims will suffer more personal harm. In the "real world," the chance of a child being a victim of sexual abuse by a predator without the use of technology is relatively low. The rate of childhood sexual victimization in 2003 was 1.2 per 1,000 American children.[6] It is challenging, however, to correctly estimate the true number of predator victims because there are many forms of victimization and because many cases never get reported. In the online world, the Crimes Against Children Research Center reported that about 1 in 25 youths received "aggressive" sexual solicitations. However, the number of youths who reported being sexually victimized by someone they met online was extremely small.[7] Still, much of the emotional harm felt (fear, distress) was due to the online solicitations that were sexual in nature, and not because of a real-life meeting.

Cyberpredators are keenly aware of the vulnerabilities of online users, and they use this to their advantage. For example, they know that young people are often online using chat rooms and social networking sites without their parents' knowledge. Cyberpredators, often sexual predators, then troll and prowl the Internet in search of susceptible young people. They are empowered through anonymity and, even more disturbing, through the ability to portray themselves in any manner that may help them ensnare their prey. For instance, a middle-aged, unhealthy man can pretend to be a young, athletic teen or can even represent himself as a young, female teen. In one high-profile case, a middle-aged female named Lori Drew pretended to be a young, friendly, "hot" teen boy. This "boy" befriended a young teenage girl named Megan Meier, but then turned on her and encouraged others to abuse her. After the ruthless display of repeated online cruelty, the distressed young teen eventually killed herself. While this adult does not fit the profile of a classic cyberpredator, the incident serves as a harsh reminder that in the online world, things are not what they seem. This can be very difficult to recognize, especially for a young person who may not have the life-experiences and decision-making ability to see the "big picture."

CONCLUSION

While cyberpredators are often considered sexual offenders or pedophiles, this is not always the case. Rather than pedophiles, who target *very* young children, cyberpredators often target adolescents ages 13 to 17.[9] Therefore, cyberpredators are more often hebephiles, which are adults who are attracted to adolescents. However, they are also murderers, stalkers, and other deviant criminals who use technology to support or help carry out their abnormal acts. For example, Michael John Anderson placed a fake online ad in order to lure an *older* woman to his home, allegedly to experience the feeling of killing. Also, while the cyberpredator can be very far away physically, they are just a mouse-click or touch-screen tap away from being in the homes of young people.

Young People
and Technology

Imagine the surprise of parents Greg and Manako Hardesty when they found out that their 13-year-old daughter Reina had totaled 14,528 text messages (both sent and received) in one month.[1] The number of pages in the AT&T phone bill was a whopping 440. Also on the bill were charges for Reina's 22-year-old sister Hana, who totaled a mere 7,101 messages during the same period. Fortunately for Mr. Hardesty, he had initially signed up for unlimited texting in his cell-phone family plan. It looks as though they certainly got their money's worth.

This was not the case for parents Gregg and Jaylene Christoffersen. They received a surprise when they saw their cell-phone bill totaling $4,756.25. The bill detailed nearly 20,000 text messages from daughter Dena in one month.[2] What was Dad's reaction to this? He smashed the cell phone with a hammer. Dena had mostly been sending these messages at school, and her grades reportedly declined during this time. Fortunately for the family, they reported that Verizon was willing to reduce the bill.

A teenager uses his Blackberry to tweet (post a status update on Twitter). (*AP Photo/Don Heupel*)

The surprise was probably the greatest from father Ted Estarija, who received a cell-phone bill for an incredible $21,917.[3] While Mr. Estarija expected the bill to be somewhat higher since he just added his son to his cell-phone plan, the actual number was likely incomprehensible. What was different about this case, though, is that the bill increased substantially after his son reportedly downloaded nearly 1.4 gigabytes of data in one month. Needless to say, the son's account was suspended.

Young people today are surrounded by technology. It is a world that they have always known, lived in, and experienced. As modern teens develop physically, emotionally, and socially, they are directly impacted by technology because it enables them to electronically communicate, play games, and share with others. When thinking about how quickly technology has assimilated into society, the phrases "exponential growth" and "technological explosion" do not adequately capture the implications. The technology has quickly spread everywhere. Incredibly, society has adjusted so fast that it seems as though the Internet and cell phones have always existed. Even people born in the 1980s, however, cannot be considered true "digital natives," as the World Wide Web protocol was not even written by Tim Berners-Lee until 1989–1990. A college-bound teenager born in 1970 began college carrying a typewriter or word processor,

YOU DO THE MATH

The stories of teenagers sending and receiving thousands of text messages or downloading huge amounts of data are surprising at first because of the amazingly high cost on the cell-phone

AVERAGE NUMBER OF MONTHLY CALLS VS. TEXT MESSAGES AMONG U.S. WIRELESS SUBSCRIBERS BY AGE (Q2 2008)		
	CALLS	**TEXTS**
All Subs	204	357
12 & Under	137	428
Ages 13-17	231	1742
Ages 18-24	265	790
Ages 25-34	239	331
Ages 35-44	223	236
Ages 45-54	193	128
Ages 55-64	145	38
Ages 65+	99	14

Source: Nielsen Mobile

at a time when simple transmissions of electronic messages were regarded as science fiction. Little would this teenager know that by graduation, four years later, society would be immersed in a remarkable technological change led by the rise of the Internet.

Does growing up with this technology boom mean that teenagers have embraced the technologies and included them in their lifestyles? Research by the Pew Internet & American Life Project indicated that the answer to this question is absolutely yes. Data from the research indicates that nearly all teens use the Internet, which totals well over 20 million people when considering the total population.[4] About half of teenagers are using the Internet on a

bill. But what does it really mean to send and receive thousands of messages in one month? Can it really be done? Data from a Nielsen study show that adults and teens alike are now more likely to text than they are to call and speak to another person.

The data show that the average number of monthly texts for a teen is 1,742. This equates to almost 60 texts per day, and minus eight hours for sleep, this equals almost four per hour. The breakdown for Reina Hardesty and her 14,528 messages equates to about 484 messages a day, which, minus eight hours of sleep time, means 30 messages per hour.

Since Dena Christoffersen reportedly sent and received most of her nearly 20,000 messages while at school, this equates to nearly 300 texts during an eight-hour school day, or more than 37 texts per hour. Some research has shown that many teens say they can text while blindfolded. There is some reason to believe that this could be accurate. In fact, research by the Pew Internet & American Life Project has shown that texting is the most common form of interaction among teens and their friends. One in three teens sends more than 100 texts daily and 3,000 texts monthly.

daily basis.[5] Further, most teenagers own at least one personal media device such as a desktop or laptop computer, and a cell phone or personal digital assistant. Still, regardless of whether they *own* technology or not, teenagers are easily able to access the Internet. The majority of teens go online most frequently at home, and they often go online from a private area such as a bedroom.[6]

While online, there are plenty of activities that can be done by young people. For example, nearly all teens have sent or received e-mail, and most visit Web sites to get information about movies, television shows, music groups, or sports/sports stars.[7] Other activities in order of popularity include playing online video games, getting information about current events, sending or receiving instant messages, researching colleges and politics, buying things, and looking up information about health, jobs, and religion. The digital activities are not confined to computers, though. For example, more and more teens now own a cell phone, and many commonly use a cell phone to send text messages. Given the current trends, the number is sure to increase. It is hard for teens (and adults too) to resist the temptation of touch-screen phones and thousands of applications (apps) that can do just about anything. The brilliant displays and touch-screen interface that enable instant text, Web, or video access with a simple touch of a finger are indeed amazing. Teens that own cell phones are usually very active communicators online.[8] Overall, teens and young people today are increasingly using all types of technologies to communicate at all times from anywhere.

The most significant Internet activity for teens, however, involves social interaction through the use of social media. Whether it is through social networking sites or through blogs, more and more teens are using the Internet as a means to connect with and to share their creations with others. Although the numbers continue to rise at a significant pace, more than half of teenagers age 12 to 17 who are online have a profile on a social networking site. In addition, nearly half of social networkers are also bloggers.[9] Through networking or blogging, more and more teens share their own creations such as art, music, photos, and

In general, teenage girls spend more time social networking and blogging than their male counterparts. (*Allan Shoemake/Getty Images*)

stories online. It has become very clear that online social networking and creativity play a significant role in the lives of teenagers today. Unfortunately, teens who are social network users and who have created content are also more likely to report being bullied online.[10] Taken one step further, those who are sharing content, especially personal content, may be inadvertently sharing information with a predator. The fact that social networking sites that barely existed just a few years ago are now so popular is a cause for concern when thinking about safety. The fact that very young people can lie about their age to easily bypass age restrictions and gain access to the sites is even more alarming when considering a cyberpredator, who may be reaching out to victims or lying in wait and watching. For example, those younger than 14 years (minimum age limit for MySpace) and 13 years (minimum age limit for Facebook and Bebo) can and do access and set up accounts on the sites, despite rules against this.

Girls and boys engage in different online activities, which could mean a greater potential for females to become victims. For example, older teenage girls are more engaged in communications and research than similarly aged boys, and also younger girls and boys.[11] These older girls are more likely to communicate using e-mail, text messaging, and blogs. Older female teens are the most likely

YOUNG PEOPLE, GAMING, AND TECHNOLOGY

Playing online and electronic games has become an important part of youth culture today. Nearly all teenagers play some form of online, portable, or electronic console games. Most gamers play many different types of game genres such as racing, sports, rhythm games (e.g., *Guitar Hero* and *Dance Dance Revolution*), fighting, first-person shooter, and the increasingly popular simulation and virtual world type games such as *World of Warcraft* or *Second Life*.

Online and electronic gaming can be a relaxing, fun, educational, and social experience. While most teens are more likely to play online games with people they know, many also play online games with people they met online. And while gaming can be a very positive experience, it has also received negative attention based on associations with violent and adult content, aggression and harassment among players, profanity, and exposing players to cyberpredators. There have not always been ways to report problems and protect gamers, but gaming sites have begun to take action to prevent harmful actions such as by cancelling subscriptions, banning people from playing, blocking certain gamers, or using referees on competitive gaming sites to enforce rules. Also, player support groups to blog, but even younger females (ages 12–14) are blogging more than teenage boys. Older girls are also more likely to browse for information about colleges, health, religion, and for the latest gossip on their favorite celebrities. Boys, on the other hand, are more likely to view and upload videos.[12] Gender, therefore must be considered an important element given young female's greater use of the Internet for social networking and blogging. This puts them at a greater risk of connecting with someone who intends to cause them harm. This is especially true since most cyberpredators are adult males looking for young female victims.[13] Teens can quickly get very

have emerged on the sites including "neighborhood watch" against wrongdoing. Still it is the players themselves who have the ultimate responsibility to protect themselves, and to make smart decisions such as leaving the game if they feel uneasy or unsafe.

A boy plays the computer game *World of Warcraft*. Such role-playing and world-simulation games have become popular, but they can expose children to cyberpredators. (*AFP/Getty Images*) comfortable using the technology to communicate in so many ways, which may be setting them up for problems due to a false sense of security and confidence.

CONCLUSION

The fact that young people today use technology as a normal and cultural way to communicate makes the dangers all the more real. Their lives often involve the routine and daily use of technology to communicate, socialize, gather and share content, and to otherwise have fun. Evidence of this is everywhere, as teens can often be seen looking down at their cell phones, punching and pushing buttons. It appears to be a *habit* for many people, as they constantly are reaching for their device to see if they have a message. Young people, and even adults, are now more inclined to text, chat, or post to a friend, rather than speak to them in person or on an "old" landline phone.

The amount of time spent on the Internet has surpassed the amount of time spent watching television for many people. Yet, despite this immersion in the digital world, which is largely unregulated and unsupervised, young people are still often not taught about how to safely use technology. Therefore, without being properly informed by adults of the guidelines, rules, and dangers online, it is important to consider safety as a guide at all times. This means that words and messages should be carefully considered before sending or posting. While online, similar to the famous police Miranda warning, which states that "Anything you say can and will be used against you . . .," words or pictures can be used against others by employers, college admissions officials, friends, and strangers alike. When information is communicated freely with strangers, one must think about the point at which unknown people are not strangers anymore. The truth is that one can never *really* know a person without meeting them, and when a real-life meeting is arranged for someone met online, the potential for harm exists in many ways.

The Vulnerability
of Being Online

In 2006, three Brigham Young University psychologists conducted an experiment that offered insight into online communication and behavior. An ABC News *Primetime* special aired the experiment that involved 11 girls between the ages of 13 and 17.[1] The girls were split into three groups and placed in separate rooms containing computers and Web cams. The researchers instructed the girls to role-play using the technology to communicate in order to fit in with another group (comprised of male college students). Shortly after the experiment began, rivalries began to form and the groups began using comments to attack the other groups. Insults and name-calling via text messages and e-mail ensued, and included nasty comments about physical appearances and clothing. Some digital pictures were also altered to make others looks bad. Despite knowing that this was supposed to be role-play, some of the girls were emotionally upset and hurt by the comments and behavior. One researcher noted how otherwise nice people can be hurtful under the "cloak of secrecy." The girls were saying and doing cruel things via computer and text that they would not do in person. In trying to explain, one of the girls said that she really did not consider how her comments would be received by others. The study demonstrated how people may behave very differently online than they ever would in person.

THE NATURE OF ONLINE COMMUNICATION

In recent history, communication has traditionally taken place in person (face to face), on the phone, or through some written method. With technological advances, there is little doubt that the communication process has been drastically changed. With face-to-face communication, individuals can observe verbal and nonverbal cues, body language, and visual feedback. This allows one to better assess the "feel" of the conversation and any associated nuances that can be observed. While online or using a cell phone, the nonverbal cues and immediate feedback are not there, and the tone of the message is difficult to "hear." Without seeing a nod or a smile, the lack of eye contact, or a look of absolute boredom or of excited interest, there are no signs to indicate what and how a message is being sent or received. This is why it can be difficult to be sarcastic or humorous online or when sending an e-mail or IM; the message can easily be taken the wrong way. Exclamation marks or smiley/frown faces may help, but simple, written words can easily be misinterpreted. Also, while online, people will say, type, or do things that they normally would not do in person.

In fact, while online, young people often lose their sense of inhibition and self-control, which has been referred to as the "disinhibition effect."[2] For example, they may find it easier to express themselves or reveal sensitive, personal information without thinking through the potential consequences. While communicating this way, young individuals are not as concerned about how others may view them. This lack of concern can lead to problems, although the disinhibiton effect may not always be negative. For instance, it can encourage communication where an otherwise shy or reserved individual may not do so in person, or it may contribute to a person showing acts of kindness. However, it can also lead to risky, violent, or deviant behavior. Young people may instantly send or post what they feel without taking responsibility for it because it was not said in person. The experiment involving the young girls certainly provides evidence of this. Of greater concern, disinhibition and naiveté about online dangers can lead to unsafe behaviors and activities such as posting or sharing too much information with a stranger.

How else does technological disinhibition increase the risk of being victimized by a cyberpredator? Cybersafety expert Nancy Willard noted how technology can create an illusion of invisibility.[3] In other words, when people feel anonymous, they believe that their identity cannot be discovered by others while online. This is a cause of concern because things can be quite the opposite. Young people, and even adults, often lose sight of the fact that their "e-circle," or electronic contacts such as friends, relatives, and co-workers, often pay close attention to what is being said or posted online. Further, while social networking, members of the e-circle may be eavesdropping electronically and may become confused or agitated over online comments. Young people may not even be aware that their messages, posts, pictures, and links may portray an image of themselves that was not intended. This can mean trouble for teens that cyberpredators may target because they come across online as "interested" or sexually suggestive.

Some young people are more inclined to engage in inappropriate or risky activities when they believe they are anonymous and will not get caught. In addition to feelings of anonymity and invisibility, other factors can influence online disinhibition. For example, one influence is the time lag that occurs with getting feedback after sending messages. When participants are not communicating at the same point in time, the communication is considered asynchronous. In other words, the communication does not take place in real time as it does with synchronous communication. Examples include sending e-mail and text messages, posting in an online college course, or using message boards. The response to a message or posting can vary in length from minutes to days or months. Therefore, this could make sharing or posting inappropriate information

Using the anonymity of social networking Web sites like Facebook, cyber-predators can create fake profiles to lure potential victims. (*Press Association via AP Images*)

easier to do given that one does not have to deal with an immediate reaction. It is much easier to click and send something risky or negative, knowing that the information may not be immediately seen or responded to.

In addition, since online interactions often occur in groups, the concept of group polarization should also be considered as a risk factor. Group polarization means that people are more inclined to be extreme in their thinking after communicating in groups. For example, people who are risk-takers in general can engage in a group discussion and then leave with an even stronger sense of risk-taking because they talked about and decided on something together. Groups often make more extreme decisions than an individual member of a group normally would. The tendencies of the individual group member are then strengthened after the group interaction. This usually happens with face-to-face discussions, but can also happen in online discussions, where participants feel anonymous and uninhibited anyway. Group polarization could apply to some types of cyberpredators who exchange child pornography. For example, they meet online in chat rooms or on Web sites to share fantasies and give advice to each other. As a group, these predators may make riskier or illegal decisions together. This in turn can strengthen the individual tendencies to engage in such behavior. Therefore, the group members seem to be reinforcing their shared deviant desires.

Another factor that can influence risky online behavior is the perception that the cyberworld is not real. Therefore, people communicating there are characters, and cyberspace is just a game. When interacting in a game world, there is a feeling that there is no responsibility for actions because it is simply a game, similar to a video game. Talking with complete strangers and having inappropriate conversations with them may be viewed as okay since it is not occurring in real life. In addition, communicating online can be influenced by the notion that cyberspace equals the playing field. Therefore, in a world where people are seen on the same level, the perception of power or authority is reduced and can lead to misbehavior. This can also lead to risky behavior for teens who are unable to tell that someone may be attempting to gain a sense of power by controlling or commanding them. Young people may view communicating online as another type of game, especially when they create avatars or online personas. Thus, the poor treatment of someone online can be attributed to an online character, with a teenager rationalizing that they were only doing what they were doing as a pretend character. The irony in this is that cyberpredators may use pretend characters for much worse than this.

Consider this statistic: The majority of male teenagers and about one-half of female teenagers have reported that their online profiles such as on a social networking site contain phony or untrue information.[4] In fact, some profiles created by teens contain information that is mostly or completely made up. What if this information is sexual in nature or is enticing others to respond or connect? This is bait for the cyberpredator. On the flip side, when done under the guise of a fabricated persona or false information, cyberpredators can also portray themselves as virtually anyone. As it is for teens, it is also very simple for a cyberpredator to create a fake online profile about themselves or another, complete with bogus information.

Other dangers may exist as cyberpredators can easily take on a character to set up an attack in real life. While research has shown that cyberpredators do not always use deception, they do at times pretend to be a fellow teen. Or, they claim to be a teen *initially*, and later reveal that they are actually older. Cyberpredators can also use invisibility as an initial strategy, as they can troll the Internet and chat rooms, undetected, while hunting for prey. Some cyberpredators are more straightforward and directly say that they want sex from them. As much false information as there is online, teenagers often believe that communication and relationships are very real, and at times they may well be. They may also not be real, and the price to pay for misinterpreting an online relationship can be tragic. Overall, the nature of online communications, along with disinhibition and the feelings of being anonymous, must be considered as significant risk factors for teens online.

FBI special agents from the Innocent Images Unit monitor possible child pornography offenders in an online chat room. The unit patrols chat rooms in hopes of cracking down on possible domestic and international sex offenders. (*AP Photo/Matt Houston*)

THE NATURE OF ONLINE RELATIONSHIPS

The virtual world can be a cloudy and nebulous place, where the line between reality and fantasy is blurred. There is so much information online that it can be very difficult to tell the difference between truth and fiction. The Internet is full of endless opportunities to find information, to add to the information, and to interact with others. With the emergence of Web 2.0, there is a new era of applications available online (from social networking to blogs and wikis) that are user-generated and user-manipulated. Therefore, with online relationships that can be easily developed with the ability to interact and communicate with others one has never met in person, it is more difficult to determine what is real. While many young individuals are friends online with those they are friends with in "real life," there are also many who are friends with people they have never met face to face. Is it possible to really know someone without ever meeting them? Are they really a friend, an enemy, or a frenemy? While frenemies are usually same-age peers, such as bullies who have taken to the Web, they can also be predators pretending to be a peer in order to groom a victim over a period of time. Think about the screen name, "alan_panda_bear." It sounds friendly enough, but this name was allegedly used by a Pennsylvania state legislative aide who was

ONLINE RELATIONSHIPS BETWEEN YOUNG PEOPLE AND ADULTS

The connectivity of today's technology has created more opportunities for young people to form relationships with adults. This raises some important questions about whether this is appropriate, or whether or not a cyberpredator is involved. The line between right and wrong may or may not be clear, as indicated with the following accounts from the Online Victimization of Youth: Five Years Later (Youth Internet Safety Survey II):

- A 16-year-old girl met a 23-year-old man while on an online gaming site. The man asked to meet her in person, and asked her to send a nude photo of herself. The girl became fearful when the man told her how much information he knew about her. She stopped all contacts, and after some attempts, he stopped communicating with her. She never told her parents about this.
- A 17-year-old boy developed a romance with a 24-year-old woman. They met on an online dating site,

accused of using Internet chat rooms to discuss sex acts with a young boy. And, in fact, the term "bear" is sometimes used to refer to an older, large, hairy, adult homosexual.

People seek out and form relationships for a number of reasons. The same is true for online relationships. For example, people may seek out relationships online because of a human need to interact with, seek rewards from, and be intimate with others. This intimacy, or sense of closeness to others, can come from intellectual or emotional sharing. Intimacy can also be physical, but this element is lacking with online communications. Young people today may also

and they began seeing each other in person. The boy stated that he had sexual, physical contact with this woman.

- A 16-year-old girl met a 26-year-old woman in a chat room, where they exchanged photos. The girl stated that she could talk to this person easily, and that her parents knew about the relationship.
- A 12-year-old girl met an 18-year-old man through instant messaging. The man asked to meet her, wanted a picture, and asked for cybersex. She never told her parents about it.

Are the adults in these stories cyberpredators? Are there any illegal activities going on? Is the relationship inappropriate or wrong? The answers aren't always clear, but the examples demonstrate that relationships between kids and adults can be questionable. These relationships often fall into a grey area when thinking of right and wrong. Also, the formation of online relationships between young people and adults comes with the potential for an adult to exploit that relationship for personal gain.

seek relationships online while looking for a sense of community. In fact, presently, it can also be cultural as young people *naturally* seek out and form relationships using all types of technology. The formation of online friendships is often made easier through common interests. For instance, friendships are often formed because of shared interests such as sports, games, or other popular entertainment such as movies. With this in mind, cyberpredators can fake and feign interest with little difficulty. Consider how easy it would it be for a cyberpredator to read a post and say, "Hey, that's my favorite team too," or "Wow, I love that song also."

Online relationships can be very different than face-to-face relationships. This difference can be magnified when considering communication between teenagers and individuals who are in their twenties, thirties, and forties. In fact, many teens have formed close online relationships with adults who are much older than them. While this can be perfectly acceptable, online relationships involving strangers can also lead to sexual solicitations or face-to-face meetings, which can be more dangerous. This presents a significant concern in light of what is known about cyberpredators. When young people form online relationships with adults, the adult may take advantage of them in some way. While the Youth Internet Safety Survey II conducted in 2005, has shown that only a small percentage of young people had formed a close online relationship with adults over age 18, and over one in four of these had face-to-face meetings with the adults they met online.[5] A small number of those involved relationships that had sexual aspects, such as adults asking for sexual pictures or having some degree of sexual, physical contact with young people. Again, these numbers are small, but they still show that it happens.

CONTRIBUTING RISK FACTORS

Forming online friendships and relationships is part of the online experience for teens. Most young people who use the Internet communicate with others in a variety of ways that can be casual or more involved. They sometimes talk with people they have

A CYBERPREDATOR WHO DID NOT MEET VICTIM ONLINE

Most cases of cyberpredation involve adult men who meet their underage victims online, build relationships with them, and then encourage or request them to meet in person for a sexual encounter. However, it does not always work that way. In 2008, a 46-year-old software engineer, Douglas R. Bartlett, from Pennsylvania, was charged with preying upon a 10-year-old girl for nearly a year by using more traditional tactics of a sexual predator.[6] He would offer her candy if she would engage in sexually explicit acts. Other video evidence captured Bartlett telling the girl that he would buy her a video game if she was willing to participate in inappropriate activity. So why is Bartlett a cyberpredator and not just a molester? Bartlett reportedly used a Web cam and digital camera to record the encounters with the girl, which he then transmitted to other pedophiles he met online using the screen name "TedBed27."

The case shows that cyberpredators are often molesters who use technology to carry out their harmful intentions. The case also demonstrates how damaging cyberpredation can be. In addition to the trauma experienced from the actual abuse, the girl was also aware that sexual images of Bartlett and her were being circulated on the Internet. In short, she faces enduring victimization. She will have to live with this for the rest of her life, knowing that images distributed on the Internet may be out there forever.

never met in person, which under the right circumstances can be acceptable.

An important issue, however, is that some young people are more likely to form online relationships if they are troubled, conflicted, or have communication issues with their parents. Therefore, these problems are risk factors that could contribute to potential victimization. In addition, young people who feel lonely or depressed may also look to the Internet for help. This can also be the case for those who are exploring their sexuality or confused about their sexual preference. While the majority of teens do not have these issues, cyberpredators actively look for those that do.

Further, many teens *voluntarily* or *willingly* enter into sexual relationships with adults they meet online. These teens may not consider the fact that the adults are committing serious crimes against them, even though they may be consenting and have real feelings for the offender. Whether or not teens have problems, cyberpredators use the access gained through the Internet to influence and control vulnerable young people.

NATURAL RISK FACTORS

Young people can be at risk online due to the nature of electronic communications, but there are also some other risks that are biological. For example, studies have shown that the brains of teenagers are different than adults in a number of ways. Specifically, the front part of the brain (the prefrontal region) is responsible for assisting with anticipation, planning, and goal-directed behavior. The lower part of the brain, on the other hand, is related to emotion and "gut response." Research by Deborah Yurgelun-Todd found that the prefrontal region of the teen brain is less active than in adults, while the lower region is more active than in adults.[7] Therefore, when responding to an event, teens will often react with an emotional response rather than a thought-out response. In an experiment, when shown pictures of faces demonstrating emotion (anger, fear, happiness, sadness, confusion, etc.), teenagers were less accurate than adults in correctly identifying the emotion. For example, when shown a picture of someone who looked afraid, teens typically said that the person was shocked, confused, or sad. The teens seemed to be using more of the lower brain, meaning that they had an emotional response rather than a more planned, logical response.

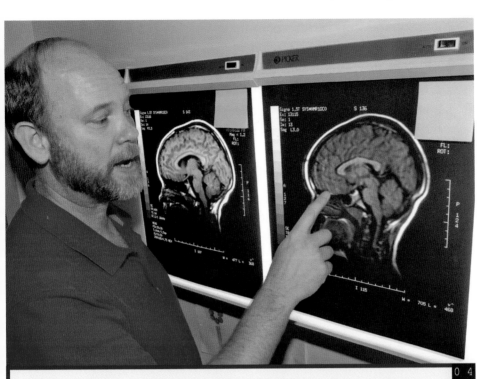

A doctor describes a teen brain scan at the National Institutes of Health in Bethesda, Maryland. Research has shown that, compared to adults, teens tend to react to situations in an emotional and impulsive manner. (*AP Photo/ Stephen J. Boitano*)

The brain research has major implications for communication, especially online communication. For instance, when online, teens may be more inclined to react impulsively rather than thoughtfully. Therefore, while communicating with strangers or getting to know someone online, they may have more difficulty telling what is real and thinking through the consequences of their behaviors. A cyber-predator may use this to their advantage and have more success in getting young people to reveal personal information (such as age, sex, and location, also known as ASL), send pictures, or meet in real life. A hypothetical thought process may be an impulsive, "this person is funny and really nice so I would like to meet him," rather than a thoughtful "this person seems funny but I don't think I know him well enough to meet in person." When other biological processes such as puberty and changing hormones are factored in, it may be even more difficult for young people to make clear decisions. The bottom line is that young people are still learning and may not make the best or safest decisions. Cyberpredators are very aware of this.

CONCLUSION: GENERATIONAL DIGITAL DIVERGENCE

One final factor that makes teens even more vulnerable has to do with adults. There is a generational digital divergence, or widening generation gap, that exists between adults and adolescents when it comes to technology. There is a gap between adults and young people on two levels. First, since teens have grown up with technology, they are often viewed as being more technologically advanced than adults. They are seen as having more skills, knowledge, and abilities in using technology than adults. Adults often think, "The kids know a lot more than me," while young people think, "My parents and teachers have no clue." Teens should be aware of this gap and make an attempt to help adults understand their online activities.

Second, and perhaps more important, young people and adults have different perceptions about the use of technology and what is *really* happening. For example, adults believe that they are supervising the use of technology by young people, while young people say they are not being supervised. Adults say they set rules for technology use, while young people say they have not been given the rules. Adults say they are communicating with their kids about technology, while kids say otherwise. Adults believe they know who their kids are talking with online and would know if their kid was being victimized is some way. Kids would say that their parents do not really know who their online "friends" are, and often will not tell the parents if they are being victimized while online. Young people will not tell because they may not believe adults would be able to help, or because they believe their parents will overreact. Young people would rather suffer in silence than risk being punished or blamed, which could result in having the technology taken away. Simply put, when it comes to technology, young people and adults are just not on the same page. Generational digital divergence puts young people at a disadvantage because of this disconnect. This divergence is yet another factor that makes the cruel intentions of the cyberpredator that much easier to carry out. Young people can help close this gap by having open and honest conversations with adults about the rules, supervision, and online safety, which can be eased by sharing positive online experiences and the latest online trends.

Using Technology to Ensnare Their Prey

Kacie Woody was a seventh grade honor student who played the saxophone and sang in the school choir.[1] She met a 17-year-old boy, David, online in a Christian chat room. David was a friend and source of support for Kacie; she often spoke with him about the death of her mother and confided in him about other issues. A friend of Kacie's described David as "sweet." David became a sympathetic ear who could identify with her problems. He also became her best friend through an online relationship that lasted nearly a year.

The reality, however, was that David was no teenager. Rather, he was a 47-year-old cyberpredator who had been stalking the 13-year-old girl. One evening, while Kacie was online, David, who was from California, showed up at her home in Arkansas, covered her face with a rag soaked in chloroform, and dragged her to a van. He then drove her to a storage unit, raped her, and shot and killed her. He then shot and killed himself.

Investigators believed that he had come to her hometown on at least two other occasions, which made the case even more chilling.

Officer Rick Woody of the Greenbrier (Arkansas) Police Department receives an award recognizing his contribution to public awareness of Internet safety. His daughter, Kacie, was abducted and murdered by an Internet predator posing as a 17-year-old boy. (*AP Photo/Mike Wintroath*)

Police believed she fought for her life while in the home, as they found signs of a struggle. They also found broken eyeglasses and were very concerned at the beginning of the investigation when they realized that she had left home without any shoes.

Kacie's father, a police officer, had known of the Internet conversations with David. He also thought David was a 17-year-old boy. Because of the age difference, he told Kacie to stop speaking with the boy. She did not listen.

E-MAIL, INSTANT MESSAGING, AND CHAT ROOMS

Many types of electronic communication applications can be used by a cyberpredator. One of the "older" methods involves e-mail.

A cyberpredator can use e-mail to directly send messages that are extremely threatening or as a way to slowly build relationships for later exploitation. Since most e-mail accounts are password protected, it is fairly easy for young people to keep the communications private. Therefore, e-mail addresses can be exchanged in another forum such as a chat or instant message, and then e-mail communications can take place out of public view.

One famous example of a cyberpredator using e-mail involved the celebrity actress Uma Thurman. The stalker allegedly showed up at Thurman's house and left a letter in which he threatened suicide if he saw Thurman with another man. He was also accused of sending harassing e-mails to her father and brother. Other sexual predators, such as pedophiles, use e-mail to send illicit and illegal pictures of children. Even more ominous, John E. Robinson, known as the first Internet serial killer, often used e-mail to communicate with his victims. Instant messaging, however, is far more popular among young people because it allows immediate, direct communication, which is appealing to anyone used to receiving instant, on-the-spot information.

Instant messaging (IM) involves using computers to send direct messages through the Internet. Services such as Yahoo! Messenger, MSN, and AOL Instant Messenger allow for immediate real-time communications. IM services usually allow for the creation of buddy lists and also enable users to send links to Web sites, photos, and music. The dark side of instant messaging is that it can also be used by a cyberpredator to immediately request information or photos or ask for a real-life meeting. Young people make it easier for the predator if they are overly trusting or willing to send personal information to strangers. Comments by an FBI special agent show how easy it is to find potential cyberpredators: "You can create a profile of a 13- or 14-year-old girl and then just go sit in a chat room and not say anything and some guy will instant message her. We sit there and let them come to us and things just start rolling from there."[2] Depending on the predator, some will IM and immediately ask for some form of sexual act, while some may pose as a caring adult who understands their issues and wants to help them. Similarly, an increasing problem is the number of adults, mostly male, who use Web cams to expose themselves to teens via Internet chat rooms. This form of public lewdness can happen in only seconds. In addition, file sharing or peer-to-peer networks allow unregulated sharing of just about anything, including child pornography.

There are thousands of stories documented in newspapers about all types of cyberpredators, from accountants to law professors, who have used chat rooms to lure underage teenage victims to meet for sex. In Chamblee, Georgia, a 40-year-old car dealer named Michael Shipman, claiming to be 17 years old, befriended a 13-year-old girl in a chat room and got her address. He then posed as a repairman and allegedly attacked her twice, raping her the second time.[3] Shipman was charged by police for rape. In Minneapolis, Minnesota, a 13-year-old girl reportedly met Joel Rensberger in a chat room, and believed he was 18. She agreed to meet him in a motel, where he gave her a video game and wine coolers before allegedly raping her.[4]

ONLINE GAMING

Online gaming is the most popular form of social activity among young people. Research has shown that children often begin using the Internet to play games when they are four to five years old.[5] While online gaming can be fun and even educational, it also provides another means for a cyberpredator to gain access to minors. Gaming forums that include basic games like checkers, cards, or chess can also be gathering places for predators searching for children. These basic games often allow players to chat in a sidebar that appears next to the game. Yet, as games have become more sophisticated, they allow players to interact more. For example, players can take on identities of different characters or engage in other role-playing activities.

Games can also provide the ultimate cover for cyberpredators who are not interested in the games themselves. Predators can troll gaming sites, looking for young targets. In the gaming world, it is very easy to portray the image of "just a gamer." Predators can chat

1103 [2:00 PM]: HI

ly [2:00 PM]: HI Craig, what's up?

1103 [2:00 PM]: NOTHING MUCH ASL

1103 [2:00 PM]: ASL PLSE

ly [2:01 PM]: 15 female fort lauderdale

1103 [2:01 PM]: COOL

ly [2:01 PM]: how bout u asl?

1103 [2:01 PM]: SAME BUT MALE AND UK

ly [2:01 PM]: really 15?

1103 [2:02 PM]: YEAH

ly [2:02 PM]: sorry, lookin for someone older

1103 [2:02 PM]: OH

1103 [2:02 PM]: OK THEN

A member of the Law Enforcement Against Child Harm (LEACH) Task Force receives an instant message. The person he is talking to (in blue) uses "ASL" to ask for the agent's age, sex, and location. (*Getty Images*)

with their prey about the game itself, and then move on to ask for information about their "opponent." For example, during casual chat about the game, the predator may ask how old the other player is or ask about where he or she lives or what he or she looks like. Young people who are into the game may not think twice about answering these questions. Also, because parents often do not associate gaming with any real danger, they may not pay much attention to these activities, even when kids are playing games late at night. In Pennsylvania, a 28-year-old man named Thay Eng crossed state lines to meet a 13-year-old girl he contacted while playing an online game. Since he met the young girl at a motel, his intentions appeared clear. He was charged with sexual assault, risk of injury to a child, and reckless endangerment. Finally, in the online gaming world, there are few avenues to report suspicious behavior, and there certainly aren't many gaming cybercops that are protecting the children.

SOCIAL NETWORKING SITES

Social networking sites contain a variety of ways to communicate and share information. These sites provide almost limitless opportunity to interact, post pictures, and socialize. After signing up, activities mainly begin with the creation of an online profile, which usually includes a picture and some personal information such as likes, dislikes, interests, and hobbies. From there, the account user can build a network of online friends that enables them to share and post information and view the contents of each others' pages. Amazingly enough, at the time of this writing, the "oldest" sites have only been around for approximately six years. What began as a mostly underground online activity during this time has grown at incredible speeds.

Adults generally associate social networking sites with the most popular sites such as MySpace and Facebook. There are hundreds, however, if not thousands of other social networking sites that fly below the radar of adults. Kids know of many of these "unknown" sites or can easily find them and create an account without their parents knowing. Research has shown that 55 percent of teenagers use social networking sites and have created online profiles.[6] About half of these users visit the sites at least daily or more. It is expected that the numbers will continue to increase as the sites continue to develop and as more people, children, and adults create profiles. This unprecedented growth has created legitimate safety concerns about how personal information can be easily spread across these personal networks. Once personal information (including messages or pictures) is posted and shared, the sender basically loses control of that information. The sites also pose safety concerns for young people as cyberpredators can use them to meet and target their victims. For example, a Brooklyn, New York, man was recently charged with having sex with a 15-year-old girl from across the state on two occasions. The man allegedly met the girl though Facebook, and during their second encounter, he allegedly recorded the act on the girl's cell phone.

Web logs, or blogs, are also very popular on the Internet. Blogs are interactive journals that allow others to participate by adding their own comments and viewpoints. Because these blogs can also be a diary of sorts, cyberpredators can search for them and read all about personal information and experiences. Whether they are part of a social networking site or not, teens often include information in their blogs such as phone numbers, class schedules, and addresses. In one case, a mother in New York had no clue that her 13-year-old daughter was blogging on the social networking site Xanga.com until officials at her daughter's school found out and notified her. She was stunned to learn that her daughter had posted pictures of herself, her age, and also posted false information, stating that she stayed out very late with her friends. Mom later found out that her daughter also had an account on MySpace, which requires users to be at least 14 years old, despite being only 13.[7]

The very process of "friending" via social networking sites creates some safety concerns. For example, some people on the sites view the number of friends as a symbol of online popularity. The more friends, the better. Therefore, as more and more people request to be their friend online, it is very easy to accept the request with little thought behind it. They may accept requests from people they have never heard of to build their friendship pool. This creates some questions and concerns. For instance, "friending" absolute strangers gives that stranger (now a "friend") access to a person's entire profile. Therefore, a predator can then visit the profile and check the posts and communications. Taking as long as they need, the predator can listen and watch, undetected, and gather all sorts of information about their friend. This is very easy since name, date of birth, and hometown are usually listed in the profile. How simple for a predator to "get to know" their friend without ever really communicating with them. They can then use that information to attack or manipulate their victim.

In addition, sites often have a feature for people to list what they are doing right now. There can be an element of danger in

ARE WEB SITES DOING ENOUGH FOR SAFETY?

Many Web sites, along with social networking sites, have been accused of moving too slowly in offering protections against online sexual predators. Still, in early 2009, MySpace was responsible for removing approximately 90,000 sex offenders from their site over a period of about two years. To accomplish this, they used technology that cross-referenced names, physical descriptions, and other characteristics of registered offenders.[9]

In New York State in 2009, more than 3,500 registered sex offenders were removed from the sites MySpace and Facebook. This was a result of a new law, Electronic Securing and Targeting of Online Predators Act (e-STOP), which went into effect. E-STOP has been called the most comprehensive law aimed at protecting people from cyberpredators in the nation. The law bans many sexual predators from using social networking sites while on parole or probation. Further, there is a requirement that all convicted sex offenders must register any Internet identifiers, e-mail addresses, and screen names with the state. Under the law, Facebook was able to identify and remove accounts of 2,782 sex offenders registered in New York, and MySpace was able to do so for 1,796 sex offenders.[10] Yet, questions remain as to whether the sites would have taken these steps if not pushed by the law.

Craigslist is another Web site that has faced pressure to clean up its act. The pressure came after complaints increased over the lewd posts and images that existed among the personal ads, many of which were blatant ads for prostitution. In addition, Craigslist was also implicated in playing a role in the murder of a New York radio reporter, George Weber, who was repeatedly stabbed to death in March 2009 by a man who allegedly answered Weber's ad for "rough sex."[11] Craigslist responded to this with a commitment to fight online prostitution. Yet, even after this, it was reported that illegal activities were still advertised on the site. Questions remain as to whether these sites can be cleaned up and how to go about it.

describing where one is going and what one is doing in real time. In recent research, 66 percent of teens who created a profile reported that they limited access to their profiles, meaning that only friends have access to the profile.[8] This is a smart and safe choice, but can only offer some protection if the decisions about whom to friend are also smart and safe. On the other hand, just about 40 percent reported they do not limit access whatsoever. Therefore, virtually anyone who stumbles upon their online profile can view all of their information.

A TEENAGE FACEBOOK CYBERPREDATOR

The case of 18-year-old Anthony Stancl suggests that teens can also be cyberpredators and that they can use social networking sites to victimize others. Stancl was accused of first contacting his victims through Facebook while pretending to be girls online named Kayla or Emily. While posing as the girls, Stancl allegedly persuaded 31 teenage boys to send him nude photos of them- selves. Victims stated that the "girl" they thought they were talk- ing to attempted to get them to meet with a "male friend" and to perform sexual acts with that friend. They were told that if they did not do as asked, then she would send the pictures to their friends online and post them on the Internet. Seven of the boys went through with the request and engaged in sexual activities with Stancl. Stancl was caught and later charged with numerous counts, including child enticement, sexual assault, and possession of child pornography, among other charges. Stancl was convicted and sentenced to 15 years in prison. If he had been convicted of all original charges, he could have received a sentence of 176 years.[14]

Another area of concern is the age requirements for signing up on social networking sites. Depending on the site, the rules state that a child must be 13 or 14 years old to create a profile. Despite this, research has indicated that among 12- to 13-year-olds, 41 percent had created an online profile.[12] These numbers do not even include the many young people who lie about their age in order to sign on to the sites. Since the sites do not have mechanisms in place for checking age, even a very young child can lie and say they are 12, 13, or 14 to gain access and create an account. Still, older teenage girls (age

Anthony Stancl leaves court after pleading no contest to two felonies. Stancl used a Facebook scam to blackmail dozens of male students into performing sex acts with him. (*AP Photo*/Journal Sentinel/*Tom Lynn*)

15–17), are much more likely to use social networking sites than younger girls or boys. While the majority of teenagers report that they use social networking sites to maintain existing friendships, half report using these sites to make new friends.[13]

Taken one step further, researchers have also found that teens who create profiles or post photos online are more likely to be contacted by an online stranger. Posting a picture can attract strangers to their profile. Once there, the stranger then attempts to communicate with them. While this contact from unknown people usually does not frighten or worry teens, those that do become concerned are more often girls. Posting pictures can also be a safety concern when thinking about technology that involves geotagging. Geotagging allows one to label or tag their digital photos to show the location of where the picture was taken (by impressing GPS coordinates into the image data). Geotagging allows people to track individuals and could be used by cyberpredators to find victims online.

Familiar questions arise: Are online friends truly friends? Can it really be known who is knocking on a chat room door? On the other hand, is it necessarily bad to be contacted by a stranger? Isn't a purpose of social networking to meet new people? A stranger is simply someone that is unknown, yet a *stranger* is often associated with a *predator*. By and large, it is unrealistic to think that teens will not talk with strangers. Therefore, current thinking has to be modified to address how strangers can be more safely communicated with. After all, the strangers being communicated with by teens are usually other teens.

CELL PHONES AND SEXTING

Cellular phones must also be part of the discussion on cyberpredators because of their increasing capabilities. Anyone can use cell phones to access the Web, where they can upload and download content. In fact, newer phones now have applications that include icons for Facebook, MySpace, and Twitter directly on the touch screen. New mobile phones also include direct access to a Web browser and e-mail accounts. Cell phones are simply mini-computers.

In fact, cell flip phones equipped with a keyboard resemble laptop computers, except for the fact that they are only inches wide. Cell phones are small, easily concealed, and quick to use. Most teens have cell phones, and those who have advanced smart phones have the world at their fingertips *anywhere or anytime.* This creates issues for both schools and parents as they grapple with ways to supervise or regulate the use of cell phones. It also expands opportunities for predators to target potential victims and creates new risks for teens.

Most cell phones are now equipped with cameras that can take, send, and post pictures in a matter of seconds. This creates another tool for cyberpredators to ask to exchange pictures of potential victims. Given the "newness" of this technology, it is unknown to what extent cyberpredators use this method. It is likely, however, that many types of child predators, such as child pornographers, are using cell phones in illegal ways. While the idea of "sexting" or sending nude or inappropriate photos usually involves teenagers, the *ages* of both parties make a significant difference as far as the law is concerned. There are numerous media accounts of teenagers (16 to 19 years old) who have been arrested for serious felony crimes involving the dissemination of child pornography. Yet, some of these cases have involved consensual exchanges of pictures involving a girlfriend or boyfriend. This does not matter, though, if one of the parties is a minor.

Should these teen-on-teen sexting participants be called cyberpredators? This really depends on the specific incident and level of harm done. Consider the case of Phillip Alpert. After having some issues with a past girlfriend, who was 16 years old at the time, Alpert decided to e-mail nude pictures of her (that she had e-mailed to him during the relationship) to over 70 people, including parents, grandparents, and school staff. A few days later he was arrested for transmitting child pornography and later was sentenced to five years probation and registration as a sex offender. In retrospect, Alpert stated that he did not realize how bad that decision was.[15] Regardless of whether he is a true cyberpredator or not, the incident demonstrates how easily modern technology can be used to harm others.

THE DIGITAL LANGUAGE

Another challenge for those who are interested in combating cyber-predators involves the language used in online and electronic communications. The shorthand language used online or for texting has been constantly changing. The initial, abbreviated language has gone much beyond the traditional "LOL," for "laughing out loud." The online language has been referred to as "netspeak" or "leetspeak," online jargon, and Internet slang. While the lists are constantly evolving, one common form of Internet slang is the use of acronyms. Acronyms may be used to communicate more quickly and efficiently. Having conversations using computers, cell phones, and PDAs can be a time-consuming and even frustrating process if everything is written in a grammatically correct way. It does not take those entering the world of text messaging via cell phone long to understand this concept. The more common acronyms such as "U" (you), "2" (too), "LOL" (laughing out loud), "BTW" (by the way), and "CYA" (see you later) are commonly used through digital communications, as are emoticons such as the popular smiley face J or variations to express emotion, such as winking ;). Acronyms can also be used as a code to prevent adults from understanding the messages or to signal that an adult is coming or watching.

Some acronyms are red flags that the person using them may pose a threat to one's safety. Common ones, such as ASL (age/sex/location), NIFOC (nude in front of computer), IPN (I'm posting naked), and LMIRL (let's meet in real life) are examples. Responding to this type of language from an unknown adult—a potential cyber-predator—can put one in a vulnerable position. The adult may not ask the personal questions right away but may wait until they have gained a level of trust. Therefore, it is more important to focus on the tactics of a cyberpredator. They will use "cool" Internet slang to further bond with young people, only to turn on them later. Further, the language itself can make young people more vulnerable in that adults may not be able to help because they do not understand the language. Overall, teens should use caution when using netspeak, as cyberpredators will be looking for or using common "door-openers" such as ASL. There are a number of Web sites that help translate the online language including http://netsmartz411.com and http://cyberbullying.us.org.

CONCLUSION

Overall, cyberpredators are increasingly using combinations of technology to carry out their crimes. Cyberpredators now have a variety of methods at their disposal to connect with their victims, probably including some that have not yet come to light.

Characteristics, Types, and Tactics

"Do you know what it means to be a slave? Your body belongs to me. You're going to serve your master every morning . . . and every night." John E. Robinson said this to victim Suzette Trouten.[1]

At the end of the 20th century, mass murders that involved technology and the Internet were basically unknown. When John E. Robinson Sr., a.k.a. The Slavemaster, was arrested in the summer of 2000, this was no longer the case. During this time, the general public became aware that the Internet could be used to support or perpetrate heinous crimes. Contrary to a rather innocent-looking image and charming demeanor, Robinson was actually a brutal serial killer. The murders occurred over a 16-year period, ending in the year 2000, and the known death toll of his victims was eight. While some of the "luckier" victims survived their horrific experiences with Robinson, the unlucky victims were killed and left to rot in sealed chemical drums.

Robinson was no stranger to the law. In the early 1980s, he was suspected in the disappearances of two females (later determined

Serial murderer John E. Robinson appears in Johnson County Court in Olathe, Kansas, for a hearing. He pled guilty to his crimes and received a life prison sentence. (*AP Photo/Matthew S. Hicks, Pool*)

to be murdered by him), but law enforcement was unable to gather evidence to prove his involvement. Rather, federal authorities were able to charge him with other illegal activities involving theft and violation of probation. In 1987, he was convicted and sent to prison in Missouri, and then to a prison in Kansas where he remained incarcerated until 1993. Upon his release from prison, Robinson discovered the Internet. He exploited its ability to connect him with people interested in similar deviant desires related to sexual domination and submission. His screen name, "Slavemaster" reflected these desires, but this deviance was much darker than simple sexual exploration.

After getting out of prison, Robinson's first victim was a prison librarian named Beverly Bonner, whom he charmed and seduced while serving his sentence. Right after his release, Bonner divorced her husband and moved in order to work for Robinson, who was always involved in some sort of business venture. She quickly disappeared and, at the same time, Robinson placed her possessions in a storage locker in Kansas City. Unbeknownst to the storage facility staff, the bodies of Bonner, along with the bodies of two other victims, were decomposing in three sealed drums in the storage locker.

The other two victims were a mother and daughter, Sheila and Debbie Faith, from California. Upon the death of her husband, the mother, Sheila, went online and attempted to meet men. It was there where she met Robinson, who portrayed himself as a rich man who could support Sheila and her daughter Debbie, who was in a wheelchair and needed therapy for conditions including cerebral palsy and spina bifida. They moved to Kansas City and disappeared shortly thereafter. Incredibly, after the murders, Robinson received a steady income from cashing government checks and alimony payments from the three victims. For years, the Social Security Administration sent checks to a post office box the victims had listed as their new address. A postal employee later testified that each month Robinson would pick up the checks made out to Bonner and the Faiths.

As technology continued to develop, Robinson became engrossed in the world of the Internet. For a period of time, his typical day involved trolling online for women who were interested in performing submissive sex acts with him. In fact, Robinson became quite popular in certain BDSM (bondage/domination/sadomasochism) chat rooms, which were becoming popular themselves. He thrived on being anonymous online, where he could shed his real-life image of a kind, grandfatherly type man. Online he was something quite different: a dominant master and charming manipulator. Through online communication, he had the ability to control people by using deception. He would lure and persuade women, often with promises of money, to come to Kansas City to live with him.

Two other victims, Izabela Lewicka and Suzette Trouten, were caught in this web of deceit. Lewicka told her parents that she was moving to Kansas City to intern with a rich entrepreneur. She actually signed a 115-item slave contract with Robinson before she disappeared. Robinson told Trouten, after meeting her through Web sites and chat rooms, that he would pay her more than $60,000 per year if she came to Kansas. Most of her e-mail and chat room friends knew she went to Kansas to work for a man known as "JR." That was the last they saw or heard of her. Some of the women who she instant messaged with daily found it unusual that she was no longer online.

It was Trouten's family that ultimately assisted with the arrest of John E. Robinson. Suzette's mother, Carolyn, grew suspicious after receiving letters, supposedly from Suzette, that were not characteristic of her daughter. Carolyn knew that the letters were not from her daughter, especially since they were typewritten and mistake free; Suzette was not a good speller and never typed notes to her mother. Carolyn contacted police, who had enough evidence to get search warrants to tap Robinson's phone and monitor online communications. For several weeks, Robinson e-mailed some of Suzette's friends and relatives, pretending to be her, but most did not fall for this. Then shifting his focus, he lured two other potential victims at the same time. While police were listening in, Robinson attempted to convince Vickie, a laid-off psychologist, to come to Kansas City, telling her that he would help her get back on her feet. During this timeframe, Vickie and another female, Jeanna, did meet with Robinson and were sexually assaulted. Finally having gathered enough evidence, police officers raided Robinson's mobile home and found the remains of five bodies in chemical drums. Robinson was able to escape a death sentence because he pled guilty and received a sentence of life without parole. Robinson never did say why he did what he did.[2]

CHARACTERISTICS OF A CYBERPREDATOR

While John E. Robinson's motives were not clearly known or understood, his case serves as an example of an extreme cyberpredator: one who kills others. His method of operation involved using technology to meet people and then using the technology to manipulate others so that he could later kill them. Robinson's predatory behavior centered on deviant sexual activities such as domination and bondage, which often involved using physical restraint or inflicting pain. Generally, the Internet can provide a forum where those interested in various abnormal activities can meet. It also creates dangerous access for cyberpredators who would cause harm to others. While cyberpredators that murder others are very rare, they do exist.

Most cyberpredators, however, are not killers. They are sex offenders that target young people. Do these predators really have a profile, or are they specific types of people? At first glance, other than the fact that they are usually men, the answer appears to be no. They appear to be all types of people with varying personalities, jobs, and life experiences. In 2001, the National Center for Missing and Exploited Children, in collaboration with the FBI, released a behavioral analysis of child molesters. In the analysis, FBI Supervisory Special Agent Kenneth Lanning cautioned that it can be difficult to identify a typology of a child molester because human behavior is complex and hard to explain. Still, Lanning identified two categories of sex offenders: situational and preferential. On the one hand, situational offenders tended to be less smart, have lower socioeconomic status, and their criminal sexual behavior is impulsive and focused on meeting sexual needs. On the other hand, preferential offenders are smarter, have higher socioeconomic status, and their criminal behavior is often compulsive and fantasy-driven. When computers are used (cases of cyberpredation), situational offenders are often impulsive and curious, have a history of violent offenses, or resort to selling child pornography to make a profit. Preferential cyberpredators are those that have a sexual preference for children and begin to act out criminally because of the opportunity afforded by online communication. Overall, Lanning's work reinforced that child molesters can be all types of people with many different characteristics.

Additional research has been conducted that focused on the characteristics of online sex offenders in an attempt to create a profile.[3] For example, the Keene police department in New Hampshire examined the characteristics of more than 200 offenders who targeted male children. Some of the information showed that offenders were mostly men in their twenties, thirties, and forties. Occupations of offenders from most to least were students, laborers, technology workers, white-collar employees, retired, youth workers, educators, law workers, medical, military, church, and those who were unemployed. Based on this, researchers created a child sex-offender typology. The first typology, and by far the most common (143 offenders), was "Collectors." This group consisted of those who collect and trade child pornography using the Internet. The second group was called "Travelers." This group included offenders who chat with children online and use deception and manipulation to arrange for real-life meetings for sexual purposes. Most Travelers were also Collectors. A third category identified was "Manufacturers." Members of this group were responsible for making or producing child pornography.

The advent of video cameras and digital photography, coupled with the rapid proliferation of computers, has dramatically impacted child pornography production. The image of a child pornographer using cameras, lights, and bulky equipment to film scenes of children has changed. The modern "Manufacturer" does not need much equipment and technical skill to produce child pornography (CP). All that is needed is the motivation and ability to find an underage victim and a digital device with a camera. The Internet has been a major contributor to the increasing amount of CP found worldwide. This is in addition to a very large, and legal, adult pornography market consisting of millions of pornographic Web sites. The motives of CP producers may be financial, if they intend to sell what they produce, or personal, such as for purposes of deviant sexual fantasy. It is important to keep in mind, however, that while CP production and distribution can be more indirect, child pornographers are still responsible for online predation because they are contributing to the perpetual victimization of children and young people. Every time an illegal image is sent, posted, traded, or otherwise viewed, that young person is victimized.

There are also two types of offender classifications that help clarify both the characteristics and tactics used by cyberpredators. The first, "Virtual Offenders," are those that engage in "fantasy only" activities that may involve experimentation in chat rooms that are pedophilic in nature.[4] They also tend to be interested in a number of other sexual themes that do not include children. These offenders are often paraphilic, meaning that they have a sexual deviation or a sexual disorder that involves intense and frequent sexual fantasies, urges, or behaviors. These offenders experiment in a slower way that eventually leads to activities with sexual themes related to

VIRTUAL OR CLASSIC OFFENDER?

A key difference between a virtual and classic offender is that a virtual offender often considers their behavior as fantasy, and they are not interested in meeting a child. The FBI defines those who travel to meet and have sex with children they met online as "Travelers." However, the line between virtual and classic offender can be blurred, especially when considering the case of Patrick Naughton. A former vice president of Disney's Go Network, Naughton was tried in a Los Angeles federal court and accused of having traveled from Washington to California after using the Internet to meet and have sex with a 13-year-old girl. Naughton's defense argued that he was only playing out a fantasy, and that he would never have acted on that fantasy but for the Internet. Naughton asserted throughout the trial that the chat rooms he visited were a source of fantasy for him. He also stated that he believed that "KrisLA," the FBI agent minors. When virtual offenders enter into these chat rooms or other areas, they are there to experiment and engage in fantasy. They are not there to actually meet young children. They are more inclined to randomly chat with different people as opposed to developing an intimate online relationship with a child. Therefore, the virtual offender would likely be arrested for possession of child pornography (a collector). They may not engage in activities that were directly harmful to children, referred to as "contact offenses."

The second type, the "Classic Offenders," on the other hand, are cyberpredators who are a direct threat to children because they are much more likely to seek out and display sexual behavior toward them. These offenders are more likely to have a past conviction of a sex offense against a minor, and they are more likely to travel to meet children they contacted online.[5] While traveling, they are

posing as a 13-year-old, was really a woman of legal age. According to Naughton, "the role I was playing was a character of me. If you ask my psychiatrist, I have a lot of self-image and ego problems. I was looking for approval."[7] Naughton eventually won a hung jury in the case based on the "fantasy defense." The jury deadlocked on whether he really was seeking to have sex with a minor, despite arranging for and traveling across state lines to meet the girl.

The case also demonstrated the difficulty in clearly distinguishing between virtual and classic offenders. Additional cases such as those of Terry Spontarelli, a research chemist from Los Alamos, New Mexico, and George DeBier, a former Belgian diplomat, also made the similar point. They were white-collar, upper-income men, with no history of breaking the law, who traveled and were arrested for meeting an FBI agent posing as a minor on the Internet. Profiling cyberpredators can be unclear, but these cases show how the Internet can be an outlet for people to explore or develop sexually deviant behavior.

likely to bring sexual objects with them such as birth control, and are also likely to bring gifts such as flowers, candy, or a teddy bear. Classic offenders are also those that try to manipulate children by posing as kids or disguising their true intentions by grooming their victim over time and building trust. To build trust or gain acceptance in a chat room, they may use screen names such as "John12" or "Claire10," with the numbers intended to falsely suggest their age. Also, they often prey upon those kids who describe themselves as "misunderstood."[6] Perhaps most disturbing, classic offenders often lack remorse and believe that their actions are acceptable because the child was a willing participant.

Other research has explored the possible psychological explanations for the behavior of cyberpredators. A study of forensic interviews with Internet sex offenders charged with sex offenses also looked at possible reasons why offenders acted a certain way. For example, some virtual offenders may be following an addiction cycle that begins with the first phase called discovery. This phase starts with curiosity piqued by fantasy-type Web sites. The next phase is experimentation. Here, virtual offenders begin in adult chat rooms, where they are exposed to a variety of themes that eventually change their views of "normal sex."[8] The next phases are escalation and then compulsion, where the fantasies may develop into an obsessive compulsion. During this phase, they become more preoccupied with the computer, and feel compelled to engage in risky behavior despite known risks of arrest or incarceration. The final phase is called hopelessness, which involves a sense of despair because they can no longer control their activities and feel disgust about their wrongdoings. This study provides some insight into why some cyberpredators (the virtual type) engage in illegal and immoral activities involving children. But, similar to the research about pedophiles and child molesters in general, the causes still remain largely unknown despite theories that explain that it could be due to genetics, poor socialization or family relationships, or being sexually abused as a child.

Additional research explored Internet sex crimes against minors by reviewing a "snapshot" of offenses that included 129 sex crimes.

This research helps to further explore the characteristics and tactics of a cyberpredator. In the study, the crimes were committed against children and began with an online encounter. The study also explored the characteristics of the offenders and victims. Most of the offenders (76 percent) were older than 26 years, while the victims were mainly 13- to 15-year-old teenage girls.[9] Most of the encounters (76 percent) began in online chat rooms and most offenders took time to develop relationships with their victims. As the relationships developed, offenders contacted their victims in a number of ways such as via telephone and through sending pictures. Many offenders also offered or gave money or gifts such as jewelry, teddy bears, clothes, cell phones, and digital cameras.

Cyberpredators can and do use deception to lure victims. The stereotypical image of a "dirty old man" pretending to be a teenage girl is difficult to change, but this is not always the case. The same study of Internet crimes also showed that deception was *not usually* used. Specifically, only 5 percent of offenders actually pretended to be a peer of the victim.[10] Also, most of the offenders were *open* about wanting sex from their victims. Still, deception was used by the offender in some of the cases that involved false promises of love or romance. Also, some did pose as a "friend," only to assault the victim later. A small number also tried to lure females by pretending to be part of a casting or modeling agency. About one-quarter of offenders did lie at some point about their appearance or other personal information.

The study also found that most of the encounters led to in-person meetings, and nearly all of them involved illegal sexual contact.[11] There were a few offenses that occurred solely online, and one case involved persuading a victim to send an illicit video. Real-life meetings occurred in various locations such as homes or hotels, and most victims met with the offender more than once. In fact, about one of five of the victims actually lived with the offender for a period of time. As for the crimes themselves, only 5 percent involved a violent offense such as rape, but some victims were given alcohol or illegal drugs, were exposed to pornography, or photographed in

THE LATEST "CRAIGSLIST KILLER"?

Philip Markoff was described as a great guy with a great smile, until 2009, when he was described as a brutal Internet predator and dubbed the "Craigslist Killer." [16] Markoff, a Boston University Medical student, was charged with allegedly contacting two women on the Web site Craigslist and luring them to hotels, where he later robbed one woman. Days later, he allegedly killed the second woman, Julissa Brisman, after she resisted his attempt to rob her. Police reported that Brisman had broken free of plastic ties that the accused had used to bind her, and then she was shot three times and had her "head bashed in." Markoff was believed to have responded to Brisman's ad for erotic massage on Craigslist. The first woman told investigators that a man (allegedly identified as Markoff) met her at a hotel, where he pointed a gun at her, bound her, and robbed her of more than $800 in personal items.

Shortly after his arrest, reports from ABC News stated that police executed a search warrant for Markoff's apartment. They reportedly found a semiautomatic weapon, about 60 pairs of plastic "flex" handcuffs, pairs of woman's underwear, and duct tape. Markoff pled not guilty to the charges. In August 2010, Markoff was found dead of apparent suicide at the Nashua Street Jail, with a garbage bag over his head and tied around his neck. While his guilt or innocence was never proven in a court of law, the case provides another possible example of how the Internet can be used to seek out, and victimize others.

sexual poses. Again, while the research shows that cyberpredators are not always violent, the level of harm and distress caused to victims is still significant.

Interestingly, this study also showed that online sex offenders may not usually be pedophiles. Pedophilia, a type of sexual paraphilia (sexual disorder), is defined by the American Psychiatric Association's Diagnostic and Statistical Manual of Mental Disorders, (DSM-IV) as "recurrent, intense, sexually arousing fantasies, sexual urges, or behaviors involving sexual activity with a prepubescent child." While the term is clearly defined in the psychological literature, the causes of pedophilia still remain largely unknown.[12] What is clear is that pedophiles are attracted to prepubescent children. In this study, none of the victims were under the age of 12. Therefore, the stereotype that cyberpredators are usually pedophiles may often be inaccurate. Cyberpredators often target minors, but not very young minors. Another inaccurate image is that cyberpredators always abduct their victims or force them into meetings and or sexual encounters. In reality, many of the victims voluntarily meet with the predator knowing of their sexual interests. This reinforces the message that young people need to be very cautious when forming relationships with strangers—especially with adult strangers. Such relationships often do not end well.

While it can be debated whether cyberpredators may or may not be *true* pedophiles, this should not take way from the fact that predators in the traditional sense *are* often pedophiles. Sexual predators and child molesters continue to assault prepubescent children on a large-scale basis. These serious crimes, often federal offenses, committed against children simply happen all too often and result in extreme, long-tern harm for kids. Cyberpredators only consist of a portion of all predators, however. They most often target minors who are older than prepubescent, meaning mostly teenagers who are not of legal age. It is important to keep in mind that very young individuals are often not yet using online social communication, and this may help explain why victims are usually older. Very young children are also supervised more by adults and are usually not yet interested in relationships. They would simply rather play games. Therefore, it is more difficult for cyberpredators to directly target very young children. Older youth are more inclined to use social networking sites and other interactive online communication methods that put themselves more at risk for victimization.

The home of Beth Loschin and James Warren in Farmingdale, New York, was used to imprison a 15-year-old girl for a week. The couple met the girl in an online chat room and offered to help her run away from home. (*Getty Images*)

Another term, hebephilia, may better explain some of the motives of cyberpredators. Although used inconsistently, hebephilia involves adult attraction to adolescents. Hebephilia, however, is not a paraphilia, according to the DSM IV. Given the age and vulnerability of victims, hebephiles, who use technology to harm minors, also fit the current definition of a cyberpredator and are usually guilty of committing serious crimes against minors.

While cyberpredators often target their prey alone, this is not always the case. In August 2001, 41-year-old James Warren and 46-year-old Beth Loschin allegedly met a 15-year-old Massachusetts girl in an online chat room. It was there where they offered her "help" in running away from her home. Instead of running away to a better situation, the girl was held in Warren's and Loschin's Long Island home for nearly a week, where they repeatedly beat and sexually assaulted her. They even brought the girl to the home of a third abuser, Michael Montez, who insisted that she follow orders or be killed.[13] The victim testified that she had been whipped, choked until she passed out, smothered with a bag over her head, and burned on her breasts, among other things. In 2003, Warren was sentenced to a prison term of 150 years to life after being convicted of 63 counts of kidnapping, rape, sodomy, sexual abuse, assault, and child endangerment. Loschin and Montez also received prison sentences after pleading guilty. While these cases involving a team of cyberpredators are rare, the harmful effects are surely magnified.

The victims of cyberpredators can be harmed despite never having been touched, and sometimes there is no actual "victim" at all. Consider the case of George T. Houde. In Stafford County, Virginia, Houde was convicted and the jury recommended that he be sentenced to 86 years in prison for trying to solicit a teenage girl over the Internet. There was no girl in this case, as the "14-year-old" was an undercover detective. The detective claimed that he had more than 20 chats with Houde over a few months, and that Houde let "the girl" watch him masturbate via the Internet. Houde stated that he believed he was chatting with a grown woman. He had no prior criminal record.[14]

While cyberpredators are mostly sex offenders, there are still others that fall into categories such as stalkers and murderers. The first "Craigslist Killer" placed an online ad for a babysitter and allegedly lured his victim in order to experience the killing of another person. There are numerous tactics that can be used that may range from a single online encounter to a long-term and carefully thought-out manipulation of an unsuspecting victim. Sometimes they lie, and sometimes they are honest about what they want. Sometimes they pretend to be another person, and sometimes they are themselves. Sometimes they use what the National Center for Missing and Exploited Children calls "online enticement," where they manipulate and coax young people into snapping compromising pictures of themselves. Whatever the

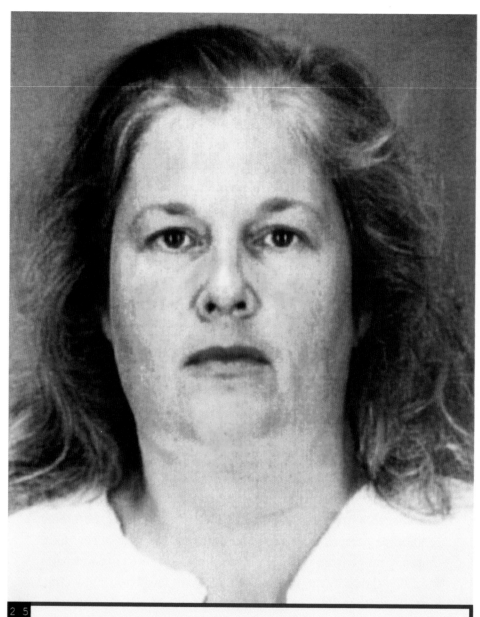

Beth Loschin appears in a police mug shot taken on August 10, 2001. Arrested along with Loschin on charges of sodomy and sexual abuse were James Warren and Michael Montez. (*Getty Images*)

tactics used, one common element is that they have more power than their victims. This may be based on their older age, ability to control the situation, or otherwise based on the exploitation of the vulnerability of their victims.

In another case, a different tactic was used to victimize a woman in 2009. In what was believed to be a first, Jonathon Hock was arrested for sexual assault and voyeurism for allegedly sexually assaulting a woman while she was unconscious and broadcasting it over the Internet at the time of the assault. Hock allegedly assaulted a woman whom he had been dating for a few weeks after she became drunk and passed out at her home. According to a search warrant affidavit, after she went to sleep, Hock went into her bedroom and set up a laptop with a built-in camera. He then allegedly signed on to a Web site, and sexually assaulted her while showing it live. He also allegedly was laughing and making comments that she would never know what was happening because she was passed out.[15] Hock's defense asserted that the recording of the incident does not show a sexual assault. Also, while the Web site removed the broadcast after it ended, questions remain as to how many people viewed or even saved the video. This further adds to the public humiliation and victimization of the woman.

CONCLUSION

The stereotypical image of the cyberpredator as a violent and sadistic sociopath is not accurate. Still, collectors and makers of online child pornography are cyberpredators because they take part in the harm of children. Other cyberpredators use the emerging technology to harm their victims. As for the reasons why cyberpredators do what they do, the causes are unknown. This is the case for pedophiles as there are a number of theories that have attempted to explain why they are attracted to children. Overall, while research may show that cyberpredators are mostly not violent or sadistic and rarely abduct their victims, they are predators nonetheless. The bottom line is that, whether they only collect pictures or also try to lure children or teens, pedophiles or not, they are still responsible for victimizing and harming *minors*. The technology does not cause a person to be a cyberpredator, but it does provide both the access and opportunity to harm others. One has to wonder if the technology makes possible for certain people what they would not have done otherwise.

Laws, Investigations, and Legal Issues

One of the first publicly known cyberpredator incidents was the case of Katie Tarbox. Katie lived in a wealthy neighborhood in Connecticut. She was considered a good student and was a nationally ranked swimmer. In 1995, she discovered an increasingly popular online activity called Internet chatting while on America Online (AOL). Katie was not very popular with boys at a time when her friends began dating. At the age of 13, Katie met 23-year-old "Mark" online. He came across as very kind, caring, and understanding of her. Katie eventually agreed to meet Mark at a hotel in Texas, where she was staying with her swim team. Upon going to his room, she was shocked that he did not look like his picture and seemed much older. Within minutes, he pushed her onto a couch and attempted to kiss and grab her in an inappropriate way. Fortunately, they were interrupted by Katie's mother, her swim coaches, and police officers.

Mark was actually 41-year-old Francis Kufrovich, president of an investment funds company in California. Prosecutors later said that he had a history of preying upon young people. Fortunately, he was stopped before anything else happened to Katie. Afterward, Katie felt victimized not only from the trauma of what could have happened, but also by how she felt abandoned by family and friends. Katie recalled how her mom screamed at her and said, "This could ruin a man's life, Katie. Do you understand?" Also, Katie felt like she had lost her best friend ("Mark"), her real friends disappeared, and she ended up having to transfer to a private school because other kids were bullying her for dating a 41-year-old. She also had to testify in court and had to take a lie detector test. Overall, the case showed that the impact of being a victim of a cyberpredator can be severe in many ways.[1]

FEDERAL LAWS PERTAINING TO CYBERPREDATORS

There are many federal laws that criminalize the activities of different types of cyberpredators. For example, cases involving sexual predators and offenses involving child pornography are covered by 18 U.S.C. § 1466A, Obscene Visual Representations of the Sexual Abuse of Children. These laws cover using computers to distribute or possess child pornography. This section involves any person who "knowingly produces, distributes, receives, or possesses with intent to distribute, a visual depiction of any kind, including a drawing, cartoon, sculpture, or painting, that depicts a minor engaging in sexually explicit conduct." Otherwise stated, it is against federal law to send, receive, or produce visual images of children engaging in sexual activities. In addition, another federal statute, § 1470, covers the transfer of obscene materials to minors. It involves one who "knowingly transfers obscene matter to another individual who has not attained the age of 16 years."

Further, § 2251 involves sexual exploitation of children and states: "Any person who employs, uses, persuades, induces, entices, or coerces any minor to engage in, or who has a minor assist any other person to engage in, or who transports any minor in or affecting interstate or foreign commerce, or in any Territory or Possession of the United States, with the intent that such minor engage in, any sexually explicit conduct for the purpose of producing any visual depiction of such conduct or for the purpose of transmitting a live visual depiction of such conduct." Therefore, it is illegal for someone to encourage or force a child to engage in sexual conduct in order to produce sexual images. The section also acknowledges that this may be done by using a computer. It is also illegal to transport children for the same purpose. There are also different sections of federal laws that prohibit unwanted sexual solicitation of children and pornography involving children.

In addition to these statutes, Congress has passed laws aimed at protecting children from harmful Internet material. For example, the Child Online Protection Act (COPA, passed in 1998) restricts the spread of "obscene" material and other material harmful to minors over the Internet. More recently, the Children's Internet Protection Act (CIPA, 2001) was passed to address concerns about offensive content on the Internet in schools or libraries. The law requires schools to have a policy addressing the safety of young people who use various forms of electronic communications. Further, federal law 18 U.S.C. § 2258A requires electronic service providers to register and report apparent child pornography directly to the CyberTipline, a federally authorized hotline for reporting suspected activities of cyberpredators.

Another law that affects cyberpredators is the Prosecutorial Remedies and Other Tools to End the Exploitation of Children Today Act of 2003 (also known as the PROTECT Act). The Act provided law enforcement tools to help investigate and punish crimes against children, and strengthened laws against child pornography. Also, the Adam Walsh Child Protection and Safety Act of 2006 gave law enforcement more resources to combat crimes against children on the Internet. It also created additional Internet Crimes Against Children (ICAC) Task Forces as well as computer forensic analysts for cases involving child sexual exploitation.

Another nationwide initiative against the sexual exploitation of children, Project Safe Childhood, was launched in 2006 by the U.S. Department of Justice. The goal of the initiative was to combat child abuse perpetrated by online predators. This has been achieved through the collaboration of federal, state, and local law enforcement to successfully prosecute cyberpredators, and to rescue their victims. At the federal level alone, the initiative has involved the partnering of numerous agencies including the U.S. Immigration and Customs Enforcement, the U.S. Postal Inspection Service, the U.S Secret Service, and the National Center for Missing and Exploited Children.

Federal laws against stalking may also apply to cyberpredators. For example, federal law 18 U.S.C. Chapter 110A addresses stalking and domestic violence. Federal law 18 U.S.C. § 875 covers sending threatening communications to people across state lines or in other countries. Further, federal law U.S.C. § 47-223 prohibits Internet harassment involving direct communications between a stalker and victim.

STATE LAWS PERTAINING TO CYBERPREDATORS

Every state has criminal laws dealing with adults who engage in sexual relations with minors. In addition, just about every state in the United States has laws against cyberpredators, which includes online sexual predators. Each state may word the laws differently, but many have laws that forbid the online enticement of minors. The laws may specifically call it online enticement or describe it another way, but what it means is using a computer or other electronic communications (such as phones) to persuade, lure, seduce, coerce, urge, request, encourage, or solicit a child to meet for sexual purposes. Similarly, many states have laws against sending indecent material, such as obscene pictures or messages, to a minor. Other laws exist to cover the exchange, distribution, or production of child pornography. Most of the laws are serious offenses that are classified as felonies.

Other state laws may also apply to cyberpredator cases depending on the incident. For example, a specific case may involve online enticement, but may also result in other crimes being committed such as sexual assault, assault, kidnapping, or statutory rape. Other charges that can be related to cyberpredators may include aggravated harassment, stalking or cyberstalking, reckless endangerment, menacing, felony assault, forcible rape, and murder. When minors are involved, state charges such as endangering the welfare of a child may apply. For example, a recent case in New York State involved a man accused of sending racy and indecent images to a minor via cell-phone text messages. The man was charged with second-degree dissemination of indecent material to a minor (a felony) and endangering the welfare of a child (a misdemeanor). Therefore, those cyberpredators arrested usually face multiple charges.

Violation of the laws can result in prosecution in criminal court, meaning that offenders are charged by a local or government law enforcement agency and then tried in a court of law to determine guilt or innocence. Cases can also be brought to civil court if the victim decides to file a lawsuit, or sue, because of wrongdoing committed by another. Victims (plaintiffs) must prove, based on a preponderance of the evidence, that they were harmed due to the behavior of another. The use of civil law and lawsuits does not appear to be common in cases involving cyberpredators. In order to prove wrongdoing in civil court, a plaintiff must demonstrate intentional, negligent, or reckless behavior on the part of the responsible party. This means that there must be believable evidence that a tort occurred *and* caused harm and suffering. For example, in Texas in 2007, a mother of a teen allegedly assaulted by a man she met on the social networking site MySpace filed a $30 million lawsuit against the social networking site. A federal judge in Texas dismissed the case, however, saying that MySpace was not responsible or negligent. In 1996, Congress passed the Communications Decency Act (CDA), which granted broad immunity to Internet service providers (ISPs) from legal responsibility for behaviors by their users that include cyberbullying, harassment, defamation, and stalking online. Basically, Internet service providers are viewed as distributors rather than publishers of information who may actively edit or monitor online content. In other words, ISPs and social networking sites are not responsible for what individuals using their services do. Still, if ISPs or social networking sites are negligent in cyberpredator cases, then it is reasonable that they may be found guilty of wrongdoing.

In 2008, New York passed the Electronic Securing and Targeting of Online Predators Act (e-STOP). Called the nation's most comprehensive law to enhance protections against sexual cyberpredators, e-STOP requires an outright ban for sexual predators from using social networking sites while on probation or parole. In addition, the law requires convicted sex offenders to register all e-mail addresses, screen names, and other Internet identifiers with the state. As a result, the information is then shared with social networking sites, which may use it to remove offenders from the service. As a result of the new law, social networking site Facebook was able to identify and deactivate the accounts of nearly 3,000 registered sex offenders in New York, and MySpace was able to do the same for nearly 2,000 registered sex offenders.[2] This is significant given that many cyberpredators visit these sites knowing that young people are there.

LAW ENFORCEMENT TACTICS AND INVESTIGATIONS

In addition to the many laws against the activities of cyberpredators, law enforcement agencies use a range of tactics to catch cyberpredators. One of their primary means is through undercover investigations by police. These investigations can be done in a variety of ways, but the main method involves police posing as young people. This is considered a proactive investigation because police may apprehend predators *before* they actually harm anyone.

Other investigations are considered reactive because they occur *after* police find out that someone was targeted by a cyberpredator. In these cases, police may pretend to be the targeted person or perhaps another vulnerable child. Police may also pose as parents who are looking for someone to teach their child about sex, or they may go undercover, posing as sellers or traders of child pornography.

Federal and state grant money allowed for a program targeting cyberpredators to carry out a proactive undercover investigation in Illinois. In this case, an undercover agent posed as a 15-year-old girl in a chat room. The agent began having online conversations with 36-year-old Michael D. Johnson. The conversations developed into explicit sexual discussions, and Johnson eventually asked the

A deputy collects evidence from a hard drive being used in a case with the Northwest Louisiana Internet Crimes Against Children Task Force. (*AP Photo/ The Shreveport Times, Douglas Collier*)

"girl" to meet him. Police arrested him in a public parking lot and charged him with child enticement, use of a computer to facilitate a sex crime, and exposing a child to harmful material.[3] Police find that despite the fact that cyberpredators may be suspicious when someone new enters a chat room stating that they are a teenager, someone often responds anyway thinking that it really could not be the police.

Over the last decade, there has been a large increase in law enforcement activities against cyberpredators. Increasing numbers of law enforcement agencies are responsible for combating cyberpredators, and each may end up catching them in a number of ways. Numerous federal agencies such as the Federal Bureau of Investigation (FBI), the U.S. Postal Inspection Service, and the U.S. Immigration and Customs Enforcement (ICE) have created specialized units focused on the problem. In addition, The U.S. Department of Justice has funded Internet Crimes Against Children (ICAC) Task Forces across the country that concentrate on specialized training and investigations. The ICAC Task Force Program was formed to help law enforcement agencies improve their investigative response against cyberpredators by giving them training and

THE "TO CATCH A PREDATOR" CONTROVERSY

In 2006 a television show joined the efforts to catch cyberpredators. That year, NBC first aired a series of episodes on *Dateline* called "To Catch a Predator." The series was very popular and the show brought increasing national attention to the issue of grown men using technology to meet young people for sex.

The methods used by "decoys" were similar to those used by police: Volunteers would enter Internet chat rooms and pose as 12- or 13-year-old children. The decoys would usually say that they were home alone, or maybe they were interested in meeting, or perhaps interested in sex. The volunteers were from a controversial citizens group that would aggressively seek out and attempt to expose online predators. The dialogue used in the chat rooms between the decoys and potential predators was often considered very graphic and sexual in nature. The conversations usually ended with the adult agreeing to meet the "child" in person.

On the show, usually within hours of the online communication, men were shown entering an address (a house rented for the show) provided by the decoys. They would be met by another young-sounding voice, off camera, that would encourage them to come in. Inside, they were confronted by *Dateline* correspondent Chris Hansen, and the men either ran for the door because they believed he was the police, or they were eager to try to explain technical assistance. The numbers of ICAC Task Forces have also been growing (there are 61 regional Task Forces), and they have formed more and more partnerships with police agencies at the local, state, and federal levels. Training across agencies has also been increasing. Other federal entities such as the National Center for Missing and Exploited Children (NCMEC) and the National

themselves. One of the men who turned up was a firefighter from New York City, and another was a man with a criminal record and history of mental illness. Yet, as Hansen pointed out, each of the men had something in common: They all used the same excuse that it was the first time they had done it, and they did not intend to have relations with a minor. For one of the shows, 18 men showed up in a period of two days.

There were objections to the program. One was that the operation was a form of entrapment. Entrapment is a legal term that involves being persuaded by law enforcement or other agents to commit a crime that a person would not have otherwise committed. Therefore, one problem was that the decoy was often the first to bring up sex and invite the men over for a meeting. Another important question was whether the producers of the show were guilty of entrapment because they could be considered other agents given that they are not the police. There were also questions about the motives of the show since its producers' primary goal would likely be achieving high ratings as opposed to trying to protect kids by having cyberpredators publicly arrested. An interesting legal question raised by the show was whether the rights of the adults were being violated because they were not being afforded due process under the law and the right to a fair trial. One target of the show, Louis Conradt, committed suicide as police entered his home to arrest him and the program's crew filmed the raid. Therefore, a key question is whether the ends of public shaming and potential arrest justified the means of using decoys to catch them.

Center for Prosecution of Child Abuse (NCPCA) also help train state and local police in areas such as undercover operations, investigations, and evidence collection.

Another way to combat child pornography is for people with knowledge about crimes to file complaints on Web sites such as obscenitycrimes.org. This site is a resource that allows private citizens to report illegal pornography on the Internet. Complaints are fully investigated and also reported to the National Obscenity Prosecution Task Force in Washington, D.C., and to the U.S. Attorney's Office and FBI bureau that has jurisdiction where the complaint was filed. In addition to undercover operations and reports from parents, victims, and citizens who happen across child pornography, police also identify cyberpredators through the direct monitoring of chat rooms and Web sites, and through connections made through other police activities such as drug investigations. Nonetheless, one problem with law enforcement is that given the multijurisdictional nature of cyberoffenses, not all the police who investigate the activities of cyberpredators have specialized training. In other words, cybercrimes of this nature occur all across the nation but not all police have been trained to properly investigate and respond.

Another valuable tool that aids in the investigations of potential cyberpredators is the National Center for Missing and Exploited Children's (NCMEC) CyberTipline. This was mandated by Congress and functions as the nation's 911 for reporting incidents of child sexual exploitation. The tip line offers a mechanism for reporting incidents involving cyberpredators, which may include the possession, manufacture, or distribution of child pornography; online enticement; child prostitution; child sex tourism; and obscene material sent to a child. The CyberTipline is staffed year-round and is funded by the federal government and corporate donors. According to NCMEC, reported incidents are investigated via a three-step process that begins with reviewing and prioritizing each lead, analyzing tips through the specialized Exploited Children Division (ECD), and then forwarding suspected wrongdoing to various law enforcement

Convicted criminals line the Wall of Shame in the Exploited Child Unit of the National Center for Missing and Exploited Children in Alexandria, Virginia. (*Getty Images*)

agencies and Internet Crimes Against Children (ICAC) Task Forces. According to NCMEC, as of October 2009, there were more than 748,927 total reports through the CyberTipline, with the majority of reports involving suspected child pornography. Also, more directly related to activities of cyberpredators, there were 46,731 reports of online enticement of children for sexual acts and 8,125 reports of unsolicited obscene material sent to a child. The large number of reports has resulted in the arrest and prosecution of thousands of offenders, many of whom were cyberpredators.

For example, in 2006, one of the major Internet service providers reported information to the CyberTipline that led to the identification and arrest of a 55-year-old California man who molested his daughter live via Web cam. Based on the information and a still image, an ECD analyst was able to search online photo albums and a convicted sex offender registry. Quickly, the analyst was able to verify not only the suspect's screen name, but also his real name, age, and possible location. Police had him in custody within hours of the initial report to the CyberTipline, and the man was eventually sentenced to 12 years in prison. Also, in another case, a report to the CyberTipline led to the arrest of a Delaware man for sending sexually abusive images of children via e-mail to a number of addresses. Overall, this investigation led to the arrest of 10 men, all from Delaware, which included a corrections officer and a firefighter.[4]

TRENDS IN ARRESTS OF CYBERPREDATORS

Getting accurate data on the numbers of cyberpredators that exist and even how many are arrested and prosecuted can be difficult to do. Criminal justice data collections systems do not, or are not always able to, collect detailed data on crimes related to cyberpredators. To make matters more difficult, there is also a "dark number" of cyberpredators that never come to the attention of law enforcement because they do not get reported or caught. In addition, sometimes those that do come to the attention of law enforcement do not get arrested or prosecuted because of legal problems. The Crimes Against Children Research Center was able to fill in some of these information gaps, however, by conducting the National Juvenile Online Victimization Study (N-JOV). The study collected data from a national sample of law enforcement agencies during a period in 2000–2001, and then again six years later in 2006. This is the only known systematic research that looked at arrest rates for cyberpredators and the characteristics of their crimes.[5]

Results from the N-JOV study showed that arrests for cyberpredators increased between 2000 and 2006.[6] Specifically, law enforcement across the nation at all levels made an estimated 615 arrests for crimes in which a cyberpredator directly solicited youth for sex and an estimated 3,100 arrests for solicitation to undercover officers posing as minors. Many more cyberpredators were arrested for soliciting undercover investigators than for soliciting actual youth.

The N-JOV study also found that the nature of the crimes committed by cyberpredators did not change much between 2000 and 2006.[7] For example, the first wave in 2000 showed that most of the cyberpredator cases involved adolescent victims who often knew that they were talking online with an older adult who wanted sex. Also, most of the charges in these cases involved non-forcible sexual crimes with minors. Incidents of extreme violence, stalking, and abduction were rare. The results from the second wave in 2006 showed similar results. For example, victims were still mostly adolescents as opposed to very young children, and most offenders were still open about their intentions. Again, in 2006, extreme violence and sexual violence were rare, and almost three out of four cases started with online communication that led to an in-person meeting and illegal sex because the victim was too young to consent. Still, regardless of whether or not physical harm occurs, these types of cyberpredators pose a serious threat to the health and emotional well-being of young people. The following case study from the N-JOV research is an example.

A 14-year-old girl and a 24-year-old male (claiming to be 19) met on a social networking site. The online communication progressed and became romantic and sexual enough that the girl believed she was in love. They met in person for sex on a number of occasions over a period of weeks. During the encounters, the cyberpredator took nude pictures of the girl and supplied her with drugs and alcohol. Eventually, the girl's mother and stepfather found out and reported the situation to police. The cyberpredator was arrested and later found guilty, and he was also implicated in another online enticement case. The victim had her share of problems, including issues with her parents and school, along with problems with drug and alcohol use. She had even posted provocative images of herself on the social networking site.[8] This is a prime example of how cyberpredators operate: They prey upon young people who are *vulnerable* in many ways.

The N-JOV study did reveal some changes that occurred between 2000 and 2006. For example, there was a shift in the type of online communication method used by cyberpredators. In 2000, cyberpredators mostly used chat rooms to initiate contact with victims. In 2006, chat rooms were used less than half the time, while more cyberpredators began using social networking sites. Further, another difference was that in 2006, more offenders claimed to be minors. This shows that cyberpredators can lie and impersonate a young person to entice their victims. Finally, another difference from 2000 to 2006 was the increase in the number of offenders between the ages of 18 and 25.[9] This may be due to the fact that adults in these age ranges may be more inclined than older adults to use the Internet for deviant behavior.

While severe violence and abductions are rare in cyberpredator cases, they can occur. The N-JOV study described only one instance where the actions of the cyberpredator involved an abduction. In this case, the 17-year-old girl was raped by a 22-year-old man after she met him on a social networking site and went to his home.[10] After she was raped, the victim asked the offender to take her home. Rather, he refused and drove her to another town with intentions of leaving her there. She then called 911 via her cell phone, telling the dispatcher that she was being held in the man's car. He was arrested and charged with kidnapping and sexual assault.

OTHER ISSUES AND CHALLENGES

Other questions are whether or not cyberpredators are increasing in numbers and whether or not the problem will become larger and larger. The trends in arrest data show that the numbers of arrests of cyberpredators soliciting actual young people increased by more than 21 percent from 2000 to 2006. Arrests for cyberpredators soliciting undercover officers increased by *381 percent* during the same time period.[11] This dramatic increase in arrests shows that law enforcement have been taking action and having success in catching cyberpredators. Similarly, police have had some success in arresting those who have the technology to possess, distribute, or manufacture child pornography, as well as catching violent cyber-stalkers and even killers. But does the rise in the number of arrests mean that the number of cyberpredators is increasing? The larger number of arrests makes it look like this is the case. Many in law enforcement believe that the numbers are quietly multiplying, with the arrest data only showing a small fraction of what is occurring. Given technological advances and the increasing numbers of people *connecting to each other* via the Internet, it is reasonable to believe that the numbers of cyberpredators will continue to rise and be problematic.

Some justice officials in Wisconsin would agree. In 2009, Wisconsin Attorney General J.B. Van Hollen stated, "I don't think that we've made significant progress at all. Our community leaders don't even know how bad the problem is. The general population has no idea."[12] As a result, Van Hollen focused on raising the profile of Wisconsin's ICAC Task Force, recruiting local police to help, and asking for more funds from the state to help. The Wisconsin task force in 2009 had five full-time agents and six computer analysts who were described as "swamped" with investigating complaints, writing search warrant affidavits, analyzing hard drives, and interviewing victims and suspects. The following case involving a Wisconsin special agent shows how intense an investigation can be.

After entering a chat room, the agent posed as a 14-year-old boy who said he was into weightlifting and the hard-rock band AC/DC. Within hours, screen name "Paul2u" sent a message asking if he was really 14. The two exchanged messages for an hour, and "Paul2u" asked the agent about his sexual experience with men, and asked for a photo. The agent sent a photo of a police officer who was also working the case. The photo was of the officer when he was 13. "Paul2u" eventually told the agent that they could "do it" in his van, and they agreed to meet in half an hour. The agents went to the location and immediately saw the van. Deputies closed in and ordered the driver to get out. Imagine the surprise of the agent when he recognized the cyberpredator as 46-year-old Robert E. Thibault, the religion teacher of the agent's child. The agent had even seen him in church that morning. A judge sentenced Thibault to 10 years in prison, which was eventually reduced to electronic monitoring because the jail was too crowded.[13]

Some difficulties associated with child pornographers are related to the incredible amount of child pornography that is available online. It appears to be growing as a worldwide problem that could be associated with organized crime. For example, a significant portion of child porn available on the Internet is believed to have originated from organized criminals located in Eastern Europe.[14] Many of these organizations operate in locations where laws against them

TECHNOLOGY TO FIGHT TECHNOLOGY ABUSERS

In December 2009, Microsoft donated new technology to the National Center for Missing and Exploited Children to be used to combat child pornography.[17] The technology, called PhotoDNA, can be used to find images of sexual exploitation on the Internet. About 20 years ago, the problem of child pornography was considered small due to a major crackdown by law enforcement. Unfortunately, the Internet provided a means for it to proliferate again.

PhotoDNA technology can help to stop the victimization once again. The technique used is called robust hashing. This process calculates the particular characteristics of a digital image, like a digital fingerprint. This fingerprint can then be matched with other copies of the same image. PhotoDNA technology allows large data sets to be searched for matches very quickly. The technology can be used to locate inappropriate images on the Internet very quickly and efficiently. In addition, once NCMEC is able to assign a PhotoDNA either do not exist or are not well enforced. Overall, child pornographers are often able to conceal their identities online because they take extreme precautions, and this poses problems for successful investigations and prosecution of offenders.

The N-JOV study (first wave in 2000) was also used by researchers who explored issues related to the prosecution of cyberpredators who targeted individual victims. Specifically, they looked at charges and evidence, but focused more on whether the victims' truthfulness, cooperation, and willingness to engage in sexual activity affected the prosecution.[15] Based on interviews with prosecutors,

"signature" to known images of child pornography, the signature can then be shared with online service providers. The online service provider will then be able to find copies of the same photos and get rid of them. The technology will also be shared with law enforcement to disrupt the ability of cyberpredators to exploit young people. Overall, PhotoDNA is an example of technology versus technology: new technology used to fight those who use technology to harm others.

Another example of emerging technology is facial recognition technology, which can detect faces and allows police to create suspect, witness, and victim databases that can be searched for matches. For example, for suspects, the facial images can be compared against databases containing criminal "mugshots." Other technology related to digital forensics is skin-tone analysis. This technology enables police to be able to quickly identify files of interest based on the percentage of skin tone contained in the images. This is based on the idea that the higher the degree of skin tone in an image, the greater the possibility that the image can be pornographic in nature.

the researchers found that if the victim was seen as not being truthful, it hurt the case. In fact, there were only two cases that ended in acquittals at trial, and in both cases the victims were seen as being untruthful or inconsistent with their testimony. Also, about one-half of the prosecutors interviewed felt that the lack of cooperation by victims hurt their case. Examples of noncooperation included hostility (belief that what happened should not have been a crime), and also the reluctance of victims to even testify (which happened in about one-third of the cases). Further, nearly one-third of prosecutors also said that victims who willingly engaged in sexual activity with the predator hurt the court case. Still, in the cases examined, 92 percent of the cyberpredators pled guilty or were convicted at trial. One-third were sentenced to incarceration, with almost half getting one year or less in jail. Twelve percent were sentenced to more than 10 years in jail.[16]

Also in question is whether or not cyberpredators arrested in undercover proactive investigations are being successfully prosecuted. Based on the high numbers of guilty pleas or convictions, and a very small number of the cases that are dismissed, the answer appears to be yes. The defense attorneys in these cases often say that their clients were entrapped by police or just engaging in role-playing or fantasy, but it's a defense that usually does not work. Cases against cyberpredators may be made stronger by the advances in computer forensics and better overall evidence that may consist of online conversations, sexual pictures, or other items such as gifts that were brought to an in-person meeting. Also, cases involving the ICAC Task Forces are usually strong because of the efforts in training and planning.

CONCLUSION

There are numerous laws, statutes, and regulations that prohibit the activities of cyberpredators or assist in the efforts to combat cyberpredators. Law enforcement has stepped up efforts and has been diligently working to identify and arrest those who use technology to prey on young people. Arrests have soared, and numerous cyber-predators have been removed from both the virtual and real-world streets. Yet, questions remain as to whether or not the laws and efforts are enough. Unfortunately, the problem appears to be too big for laws and police to catch all cyberpredators. Improved technology such as PhotoDNA can help, but ultimately, the most effective way to face the problem is through prevention and education. The best way to battle cyberpredators is to prevent them from committing crimes and causing harm in the first place. The police and tip lines help, but are often reactive to crimes after the fact. Therefore, the important job of protection often falls to young people, in general, and the decisions they make while using technology.

Using Knowledge
for Protection:
Online Self-Defense

Case upon case of cyberpredation committed by trusted, professional adults are proof that cyberpredators do not fit a particular profile. A Pennsylvania state police officer was recently charged with criminal solicitation to rape, solicitation to statutory sexual assault, and other related charges. He was allegedly using a state-issued laptop computer to solicit an undercover officer, where he discussed meeting the undercover officer (posing as an adult) and her two daughters (made-up girls ages 8 and 10) for sexual purposes. In another recent case, an army staff sergeant was charged and sentenced for using a Web cam to stream online live sexual acts, which he displayed to an undercover officer posing as a 14-year-old. Also, a 33-year-old woman pled guilty to federal charges including conspiracy to produce child pornography, conspiracy to transport minors to engage in criminal sexual activity, aggravated sexual abuse, and other charges. The woman had introduced an unclothed minor to another codefendant during an Internet chat. She also traveled to a hotel with two children and engaged in illegal activities

A student at the Rochester Institute of Technology in Henrietta, New York, keeps his contacts limited on Twitter. For the sake of safety, it is important to exercise caution when sharing information online and allowing others access to such information. (*AP Photo/ Don Heupel*)

with them. The list goes on and on, and includes documented cases of mayors, priests, and teachers, as well as habitual sex offenders and other criminals.

Cyberpredators can be anyone, and their actions can involve a number of criminal behaviors. There are many types of cyberpredators, ranging from nonviolent sex offenders who lure children into a meeting, to people who collect or produce and distribute child pornography. Cyberpredators can also be violent stalkers, robbers, and murderers. The common thread throughout all cyberpredation cases is that they involve using technology to commit serious crimes against *vulnerable* persons. Another key element is the personal harm and destruction of well-being done to the victim of a cyberpredator. So how can people protect themselves against being harmed? The answer is by learning *online self-defense*.

Self-defense when using technology is very similar to self-defense in general. It involves using the most important and powerful weapon that exists: the brain. It involves making good decisions in order to protect oneself and reduce the opportunity to be victimized. In the age of technology, it means taking the power away from a cyberpredator by learning how to avoid becoming their prey.

The first rule of online self-defense is to "know the potential dangers and pitfalls of online and electronic interactions." The Internet of today is increasingly interactive, and provides an environment in which people can actively contribute to what is online. The Internet is a remarkable environment that has significant value for education, entertainment, information gathering and sharing, and socializing. The very nature of online communication puts people in direct contact with people they already know and with people that they do not know in person. Many cyberpredators use this aspect of the Internet to seek out and find victims, establish trust, build a relationship, introduce the topic of sex, and arrange for an in-person meeting. Chat rooms are usually the first place that people think of when they consider cyberpredators. This has been a common place for young people to receive contact from a cyberpredator since it allows for immediate communication. Other means of online interactions that could increase vulnerability for being a victim of a cyberpredator include instant messaging, blogs, online gaming, and social networking sites. All of these have been used by cyberpredators as a means to get to their victim.

Social networking sites combine aspects of many of the others, and allow users to create profiles displaying personal information, and allow for posting information and "friending" others. While it is unknown as to whether social networking site users are more likely to be a victim of a cyberpredator, the ever-increasing numbers of young people signing up on the sites means greater exposure to unknown individuals. Since the sites allow for connectivity to strangers, the dangers and pitfalls can arise when young people talk about sex with strangers, routinely "friend" people they do not know, or post personal or revealing information or pictures. Therefore, effective self-defense involves being careful about the kind of information that is posted and shared, and with whom it is being shared. Posted information can be viewed by others, and can be both permanent and forever.

The discussion about the dangers and pitfalls of online and electronic communication must include cell phones. Cell phones allow for the transmission of pictures and messages, and increasingly enable people to browse the Internet, use social networking sites and watch videos, and also play games, to name a few. Therefore, the potential for victimization by cyberpredators is very real. Overall, the first rule of online self-defense means having online *situational awareness*. This means having an understanding of what is really going on in the online environment, and trusting instincts if something does not seem "right."

The second rule in online self-defense against cyberpredators is to "know thy enemy." This includes recognizing that *cyberpredators are very real in that they exist, but they are often not what one would expect.* The image of a shady, evil cyberpredator lurking in the dark shadows of the Internet has raised fears that the Internet is not safe and that using the Internet will result in violence. While this image is usually not accurate, the reality is that *young people can be and are victimized by cyberpredators.*

One should have a sense of educated paranoia when using technology. This means knowing that there is a dark side to technology use and that cyberpredators can be people who are considered trusted adults. Be wary not only of the frightening sociopath, but of the nice guy who seems too good to be true. If it seems too good to be true, then it is. A famous quote from Sun Tzu, who wrote *The Art of War*, begins with, "Know thy self, know thy enemy." Thy enemy could be pretending to be thy friend.

The third rule of online self-defense against cyberpredators is to "know thy self." Most young people are now connected to the Internet and are increasingly using the Internet to connect and interact with others. Young people are also increasingly using cell phones and other "do-it-all" devices to connect. While this technological growth and availability can be very positive, potential victimization by cyberpredators is a challenge that must be faced. Therefore, to better protect oneself, it is important to look inward and understand personal limitations and weaknesses. This is crucial

CRIMES AGAINST CHILDREN RE-SEARCH CENTER: GETTING IT RIGHT

After conducting various studies related to online sexual predators, the Crimes Against Children Research Center (CACRC) cautions against overstating the problems related to cyberpredators. For example, based on their findings, researchers felt that the publicity regarding cyberpredators was not accurate. Specifically, cyberpredators were portrayed as violent stalkers and pedophiles who forcibly raped their victims. CACRC researchers, however, found that a more accurate model of online predators would be closer to statutory rape. In other words, most online sex offenses involve adult men who use the Internet to develop relationships and seduce underage teenagers. While acknowledging that this is still very serious, researchers found that violence and abductions were pretty rare. In order to make safety suggestions more consistent with the new knowledge, they cite more appropriate statistics and advice for young people to consider:

- In one year, 1 in 25 youth received an online sexual solicitation in which the solicitor tried to make an offline contact.

because cyberpredators target those weaknesses and use them to their advantage. First, young people must recognize that they are at a disadvantage because of lack of life experience. Life experience can help in making reasonable decisions when someone "learns the hard way." Through life experience, people realize what needs to be done differently in the future to avoid negative results. Therefore, as part of online self-defense, young people need to *trust their instincts.* If it looks or feels suspicious, then something could be very wrong and the relationship should be ended.

- Internet offenders manipulate young people into criminal sexual relationships by appealing to young people's desire to be appreciated, understood, take risks, and find out about sex.
- Internet offenders target teens who are willing to talk about sex online.
- Be careful about giving out personal information and what kinds of things are shared online.
- Be very careful with social networking sites and personal Web pages.
- Although most victims go voluntarily to meet and have sex with Internet offenders, these are nonetheless serious sex crimes that take advantage of inexperienced and vulnerable young people.
- Using the Internet or cell phone to send sexual pictures of one's self or friends can result in trouble with the law.
- Do not let friends influence one's better judgment when online together.

Source: Crimes Against Children Research Center "Fact Sheet": available at http://www.unh.edu/ccrc/internet-crimes/safety_ed.html

Part of "knowing thy self" is knowing that adolescence is a time of great change, emotional development, and developing maturity. As young people transition into adulthood, there are issues related to sexual development that relate to dating, growing curiosity, and experimentation. This can be problematic when considering online interactions with potential cyberpredators. Research has shown that relationships between victims and cyberpredators were usually unknown to others and took place in isolation. This isolation can allow the relationship to develop at a very fast pace and lead to sharing much personal information. The predator intentionally moves the relationship along very quickly while playing with the emotions of victims.

It can be very hard to be a teen. Some young people have an even tougher time and may be considered "high risk" because of problems with their parents or a history of abuse. Research has shown that "high-risk" young people are more likely to receive an aggressive online solicitation.[1] Cyberpredators are often looking for those that are "high risk" because they believe they are easier targets and know that they can manipulate the relationship by "helping." In addition, girls are more vulnerable and at risk of being a victim of a cyberpredator. Yet, most young people could be considered "high risk" because of disinhibition; they will say and do online what they would not do in person. Therefore, as part of "knowing thy self," teens should be reflective and consider the types of risks that they are taking online. In addition, when making decisions while online, they should consider the question, "How could what is said and done online be used against me?" People, young and old, often feel that nothing bad can happen to them. An important component of online self-defense is to realize that anyone and everyone can be vulnerable. This is especially true online where the truth can be hard to figure out.

The fourth rule of electronic self-defense is to "know that one is not alone." While it is very important that individuals do all they can to protect themselves online, sometimes things cannot be handled alone. Making this more difficult, when it comes to technology,

The CyberTipline handles leads from individuals reporting the sexual exploitation of children. (*Getty Images*)

there is a gap between young people and adults, meaning that they do not always see things the same way. It is important to bridge this gap to open the lines of communication and build trust. This is a two-way street, which means that both young people and adults must learn to discuss issues of online safety with each other, and to learn to embrace the technology *together*.

Whether the conversation is between parents and their children or between a young person and a trusted adult such as a teacher or coach, all can benefit from talking with and learning from each other. Anyone who feels unsafe should tell an adult and get some help, perhaps even from the police. If something just isn't right with an online communication, or if something seems inappropriate or illegal, then let someone know. The reality is that conversations with cyberpredators will often focus on sex or will involve some form of an adult "coming on" to a young person in a romantic way. While it may be alright to connect with others and even seek out romance, it is wrong for adults to take advantage of people who do not know their true intentions. Therefore, consider talking with *known, real, in-person* friends about uncomfortable or suspicious situations. Real friends are there to help and could offer reasonable advice because they are not directly involved.

Finally, the fifth rule of online self-defense is to "know that online safety is ultimately a PERSONAL responsibility." That is the essence of online self-defense. It is really about online self-empowerment and understanding the importance of individual responsibility to make good decisions. These decisions should

PROTECTING THOSE WHO ARE UNABLE TO PROTECT THEMSELVES

Online self-defense can help young individuals to avoid being victimized by focusing on self-empowerment through smart online choices. It often cannot help very young children, however, who are victimized through child pornography. That is why the efforts of state and federal law enforcement agencies are so important to protect kids and identify and prosecute offenders. One such effort, "Operation Nest Egg," launched in 2008, was a three-year federal investigation based out of the U.S. Attorney's Office for the Southern District of Indiana. Immigration and postal officials, along with state and local police, were also part of the investigation. During the investigation, federal agents focused on nearly 1,000 people from the United States and other countries who were trading millions of sexually explicit images of children. Assistant U.S. Attorney Steven D. DeBrota called the effort, "the be based on the knowledge gained about cyberpredators in general and also on some online "common sense." To help ensure safety, there are five steps that should be taken to achieve online self-empowerment:

1. **Think and think again before sending, posting, or sharing online.** Think about *who* will see it, *how* it will be seen, and *how* it "can and will be used against you." Be self-aware and mindful of disinhibition and how easy it is to say or do things online that one would not ordinarily say or do. One should not harass others online or go along with people who are acting inappropriately online.

largest crimes against children case brought anywhere by anyone."[2]

Ringleaders of the group ran a password-protected Web site and used a hierarchical system where people were ranked and had various levels of access. Group members mostly only knew each other by their screen names, and some officials described the site as a social networking site for child pornographers. While on the site, members gathered to discuss and share child pornography, and to help each other traffic the images. Overall, since the beginning of the effort, more than 50 people have been arrested across the United States, with 26 more arrested in 2010. Suspects from many other countries, including France, Germany, and England are currently being sought. Officials stated that most of the images were from Europe, and only 16 victims had been identified. This international child pornography ring was mostly not responsible for producing and making the material, but some members were alleged to have personally, sexually abused children, and recorded images. While other organized rings continue to exist, the investigation will have an impact by protecting children and bringing perpetrators to justice.

2. **Exercise some "educated paranoia" when using interactive technology.** Be very cautious when using social networking sites, online gaming, blogs, chats and other forums that allow for communication with people who may wish to cause harm. This also involves using caution when downloading free things, or engaging in other file-sharing such as via peer-to-peer.

3. **Know the law.** Adults who communicate online with young people about sex or send them indecent material via the Internet or cell phone are committing a serious crime. Older teens are considered adults in the eyes of the law. Some may be predators, or some may inadvertently send inappropriate pictures of a girlfriend who is considered a legal minor, meaning that they are committing a serious crime.

4. **Consider the "reality" of online relationships.** Can one really know a stranger while online? Can one trust that the real person behind the screen name is who they say they are? Knowing that people often act different while online, how different is that interesting person that has just been met online? What if someone is openly telling a young person that they are in their twenties, thirties, or forties and they want a relationship with them? Keeping all of this in mind, is it in one's best interests to meet with someone you met online? If a meeting happens, are friends and parents coming along? These are tough questions for sure, but they are questions that should be considered at all times.

5. **When in doubt, report it.** While this can be a difficult thing to do, it is the smart thing. Knowing online self-defense does not mean automatic protection against everyone. Save all the evidence, and get someone involved. Depending on the level of threat and who offers the best option, there are many willing to help. Do not hesitate

to contact parents; a trusted friend or adult; the Cyber-Tipline; the Internet service provider, Web site, or cell-phone provider; or the police.

CONCLUSION

Technology has many amazing things to offer and can be used in many interesting and informative ways. While it also serves to directly connect people of all ages from all across the world, there is still a *distance* that exists due to the lack of real-world contact. Cyberpredators depend on this distance to carry out their intentions. In order to protect young people, most countries have strong laws that prohibit the various activities of cyberpredators. Criminal courts routinely impose very severe prison sentences for offenders. However, as much as the criminal justice system does to catch cyberpredators and to deter others from being cyberpredators, there is no way to eliminate the overall threat. Therefore, it is crucial in today's digital world to learn as much as possible about how to safely navigate through this world. As the old saying goes, "Knowledge is power." This certainly applies to safe Internet usage. The more safety strategies one knows, the more power one has to defeat cyberpredators, who believe that they have the power to control others. This knowledge means paying attention to how the Internet is being used and to all the people being interacted with. Knowing the potential harm that exists should always serve as a guide to safe, smart online decision-making.

1995 Thirteen-year-old Katie Tarbox agrees to meet in person with a 23-year-old man she met and developed a relationship with on the Internet. The individual turns out to be a 41-year-old man with a history of preying on young people. Katie later became known as the first victim in the United States to successfully prosecute an Internet predator.

1996 Congress passes the Communications Decency Act (CDA), which grants broad immunity to Internet service providers (ISPs) from legal responsibility for behaviors that include cyberbullying, harassment, defamation, and stalking online.

1998 The Office of Juvenile Justice and Delinquency Prevention (OJJDP) initiates the Internet Crimes Against Children (ICAC) Task Force Program, a national effort aimed at combating the sexual exploitation of children via the Internet.

The National Center for Missing and Exploited Children launches the CyberTipline. This offers a mechanism for reporting incidents involving cyberpredators, which includes a number of crimes.

1999 Twenty-year-old Amy Boyer is stalked and killed by a cyberpredator while she is in her car.

2000 John E. Robinson Sr. is arrested and becomes known as the first Internet serial killer.

The National Juvenile Online Victimization Study (N-JOV) study is conducted, which involves collecting data from a national sample of law enforcement agencies during a period in 2000–2001, and then again six years later in 2006. This is the only known systematic research that looked at arrest rates for cyberpredators and the characteristics of their crimes.

The Crimes Against Children Research Center releases the results of a pioneering study about youth online safety in a report titled *Online Victimization: A Report on the Nation's Youth*. The study, also called the *Youth Internet Safety Survey (YISS 1)*, is funded by Congress through a grant to the National Center for Missing and Exploited Children.

2001   The Children's Internet Protection Act is enacted to address concerns about offensive content on the Internet in schools or libraries. The law requires schools to have a policy addressing the safety of young people who use various forms of electronic communications.

2002   Thirteen-year-old Christina Long of Danbury, Connecticut, becomes the first confirmed death by a sexual cyberpredator in the United States.

Kacie Woody, a seventh grade honor student, is shot and killed by a 47-year-old cyberpredator who manipulated her online for more than a year by pretending to be a 17-year-old boy.

2003   Prosecutorial Remedies and Other Tools to End the Exploitation of Children Today Act (also known as PROTECT Act) is enacted. The Act provides law enforcement tools to help investigate and punish crimes against children and strengthens laws against child pornography.

2004   The National Center for Missing and Exploited Children reports a 39 percent increase in the number of reported incidents of child pornography.

2006   NBC airs a series of episodes, called "To Catch a Predator," on *Dateline*. They run for approximately two years.

Three Brigham Young University psychologists conduct an experiment on cyberbullying that offers insight into online communication and behavior.

The Adam Walsh Child Protection and Safety Act is enacted to specifically give law enforcement more resources to combat crimes against children on the Internet. It also creates additional Internet Crimes Against Children (ICAC) Task Forces as well as computer forensic analysts for cases involving child sexual exploitation.

The Crimes Against Children Research Center, releases the results of part II of a pioneering study about youth online safety in a report titled *Online Victimization of Youth: Five Years Later*. Also called the *Youth Internet Safety Survey (YISS 2)*, the goal of the research was to reassess how the problems regarding online safety had changed since the first study.

2008 The Electronic Securing and Targeting of Online Predators Act (e-STOP) is passed in New York State. Called the nation's most comprehensive law to enhance protections against sexual cyberpredators, e-STOP requires convicted sex offenders to register all e-mail addresses, screen names, and other Internet identifiers with the state.

2009 Twenty-year-old Michael John Anderson is convicted of first-degree premeditated murder for the shooting death of 24-year-old Katherine Ann Olson in 2007. Anderson ran a phony ad on the Web site Craigslist, seeking a babysitter. Olson responded to the ad and met Anderson in his home, where he fatally shot her in the back.

Philip Markoff is dubbed the "Craigslist Killer." Markoff, a Boston University Medical student, is charged with allegedly contacting two women on the Web site Craigslist and luring them to hotels where he later robbed one of them. Just days later, he allegedly killed the second woman, Julissa Brisman.

The popular social networking site MySpace removes approximately 90,000 sex offenders from its site over a period of about two years.

Microsoft donates new technology to the National Center for Missing and Exploited Children that may be used to combat child pornography. The technology, called PhotoDNA, can be used to find images of sexual exploitation on the Internet.

2010   "Operation Nest Egg," a three-year federal investigation based out of the U.S. Attorney's Office for the Southern District of Indiana, breaks up a child pornography ring that was called the largest of its kind. Twenty-six people were arrested in 2010, and more than 50 people had been arrested since 2008 for accessing or trading sexually explicit images of children.

●●● ENDNOTES ●●●

INTRODUCTION

1. Katiesplace.org, "Christina's Story," Katiesplace.org, http://www.katiesplace.org/christina/christinas_story.html (Accessed August 30, 2009).

2. Rome Neal, "Internet Murder: Tips Every Parent Should Know," CBSNews.com, http://www.cbsnews.com/stories/2003/05/07/earlyshow/living/parenting/main552841.shtml (Posted May 8, 2003).

3. Samuel C. McQuade, *RIT Survey of Internet and At-Risk Behaviors* (Rochester, N.Y.: Rochester Institute of Technology, 2008).

4. CBS News, "An Online Tragedy," CBSNews.com, http://www.cbsnews.com/stories/2000/03/23/48hours/main175556.shtml (Accessed August 10, 2009).

CHAPTER 1

1. CBS News, "Craigslist Killer Gets Life Without Parole," CBSNews.com, http://www.cbsnews.com/stories/2009/04/01/national/main4911771.shtml (Accessed January 1, 2010).

2. Paul Lepkowski, "Denial of Service Attacks," *Encyclopedia of Cybercrime* (Santa Barbara, Calif.: Greenwood Press, 2009), 64.

3. Elinor Mills, "DoS Attack on Twitter Targeted Specific User," *Cbs2.com*, http://cbs2.com/business/social.media.

attack.2.1119244.html (Posted August 7, 2009).

4. Samuel C. McQuade, "Fraudulent Schemes and Theft Online," *Encyclopedia of Cybercrime*, (Santa Barbara, Calif.: Greenwood Press, 2009), 74.

5. Samuel C. McQuade, James P. Colt, and Nancy B.B. Meyers, *CyberBullying: Protecting Kids & Adults from Online Bullies* (Santa Barbara, Calif.: Praeger, 2009), 1.

6. Emily Douglas and David Finkelhor, "Childhood Sexual Abuse Fact Sheet," May 2005, http://www.unh.edu/ccrc/factsheet/pdf/childhoodsexualabusefactsheet.html (Accessed February 2, 2010).

7. Janis Wolak, David Finkelhor, and Kimberly Mitchell, "1 in 7 Youth: The Statistics about Online Sexual Solicitations," Crimes Against Children Research Center, http://www.unh.edu/ccrc/internet-crimes/factsheet_1in7.html (Accessed March 11, 2010).

8. Bill Hewitt, Siobhan Morrissey, and Pam Grout, "Did Cruel Hoax Lead to Suicide?" *People* 68, no. 23 (December 3, 2007): 135–136.

9. David Finkelhor and Kimberly Mitchell, "Internet-initiated Sex Crimes Against Minors: Implications for Prevention Based on Findings from a National Study," *Journal of Adolescent Health* 35, no. 5 (November 2004): 11–20.

10. Penny Cockerell, "Cyber Predators Target Children," *Knight Ridder Tribune Business News,* May 21, 2006.

CHAPTER 2

1. Greg Hardesty, "My Daughter Racked up 14,528 Text Messages in One Month," *Orange County Register.com*, http://www.ocregister.com/news/text-185518-phone-texting.html?pic=6 (Posted January 7, 2009).

2. Adam Chodak, "Dad Hammers Wyo. Teen's Phone after Mega-Bill," *Denverpost.com*, http://www.denverpost.com/breakingnews/ci_12097656 (Posted April 8, 2009).

3. Associated Press, "Teen Runs up Dad's Cell Bill to Nearly $22,000," MSNBC.com, http://www.msnbc.msn.com/id/34445748/ns/technology_and_science-tech_and_gadgets/ (Accessed January 23, 2010).

4. Amanda Lenhart, Mary Madden, Alexandra Macgill, and Aaron Smith, "Teens and Social Media," *Pew Internet & American Life Project*, http://www.pewinternet.org/Reports/2007/Teens-and-Social-Media.aspx (Accessed June 25, 2010).

5. Amanda Lenhart, Mary Madden, and Paul Hitlin, "Teens and Technology," *Pew Internet & American Life Project*, http://www.pewinternet.org/Reports/2005/Teens-and-Technology.aspx (Accessed June 25, 2010).

6. Lenhart, Madden, and Hitlin, 2005.

7. Lenhart, Madden, and Hitlin, 2005.

8. Lenhart, Madden, and Hitlin, 2005.

9. Lenhart, Madden, Macgill, and Smith, 2007.

10. Amanda Lenhart, "Cyber Bullying and Online Teens," *Data Memo From Pew Internet & American Life Project,* (June 27, 2007), 1, http://www.pewinternet.org/~/media/Files/Reports/2007/PIP%20Cyberbullying%20Memo.pdf.pdf (Accessed June 4, 2008).

11. Lenhart, Madden, and Hitlin, 2005.

12. Lenhart, Madden, Macgill, and Smith, 2007.

13. Janis Wolak, David Finkelhor, and Kimberly Mitchell, "Trends in Arrests of 'Online Predators.'" *Crimes Against Children Research Center,* http://www.unh.edu/ccrc/pdf/CV194.pdf (Accessed June 25, 2010).

CHAPTER 3

1. ABC News *Primetime: Cyberbullying*, ABC News Productions, 2006, DVD.

2. John Suler, "The Online Disinhibition Effect," *CyberPsychology and Behavior*, 7, no. 3 (July 28, 2004): 321–326.

3. Nancy Willard, *Cyberbullying and Cyberthreats: Responding to the Challenge of Online Social Cruelty, Threats, and Distress*, (Eugene, Oregon: Center for Safe and Responsible Internet Use, 2006).

4. Amanda Lenhart and Mary Madden, "Teens, Privacy, and Online Social Networks." *Pew/Internet and American Life Project,* http://www.pewinternet.org/Reports/2007/Teens-Privacy-and-Online-Social-Networks.aspx (Accessed June 25, 2010).

5. Janis Wolak, Kimberly Mitchell, and David Finkelhor, "Online Victimization of Youth: Five Years Later," *National Center for Missing and Exploited Children,* 2006, http://www.missingkids.com/en_US/publications/NC167.pdf (Accessed June 25, 2010).

6. Michael Hinkelman, "Perv Gets 13 1/2 Years for Yearlong Abuse of 10-Year-Old Girl," *McClatchy Business News,* July 15, 2008.

7. Deborah Yurgelun-Todd, "Inside the Teenage Brain," *PBS.org,* http://www.pbs.org/wgbh/pages/frontline/shows/teenbrain/interviews/ (Posted April 5, 2008).

CHAPTER 4

1. Christine Loftus, "Teen Murdered by Man She Met in Chatroom," *Netsmartz.org,* http://www.netsmartz.org/news/Dec02-02.htm/ (Posted December 2, 2002).

2. Penny Cockerell, "Cyber Predators Target Children," *Knight Ridder Tribune Business News,* May 21, 2006.

3. Jen Stadler, "Online Child Molesters," *Netsmartz.org,* http://www.netsmartz.org/news/onlinemolesters.htm (Posted November 14, 2009).

4. Stadler, "Online Child Molesters," 2009.

5. Samuel C. McQuade, *RIT Survey of Internet and At-Risk Behaviors* (Rochester, N.Y.: Rochester Institute of Technology, 2008).

6. Amanda Lenhart and Mary Madden. "Teens, Privacy, and Online Social Networks," *Pew/Internet and American Life Project,* http://www.pewinternet.org/Reports/2007/Teens-Privacy-and-Online-Social-Networks.aspx (Accessed June 25, 2010).

7. Jessi Hempel, "Protecting Your Kids from Cyber-Predators," *Business Week,* http://www.businessweek.com/magazine/content/05_50/b3963015.htm (Accessed July 11, 2009).

8. Lenhart and Madden, 2007.

9. Associated Press, "MySpace Removes 90,000 Sex Offenders," MSNBC.com, http://www.msnbc.com/id/28999365/ns/technology_and_science_security/# (Accessed June 6, 2009).

10. Thedailyreview.com, "E-Stop Law Purges NY Sex Offenders from Facebook and MySpace," Thedailyreview.com, http://thedailyreview.com/news/e-stop-law-purges-ny-sex-offenders-from-facebook-and-myspace-1.457378?localLinksEnabled=false (Accessed December 5, 2009).

11. Billy Parker, "Teen Murderer of Radio Newsman Has Haunting Web Trail," Gothamist, http://

gothamist.com/2009/03/25/ teen_murder_of_radio_news man_left.php (Accessed August 1, 2009).

12. Lenhart and Madden, 2007.

13. Lenhart and Madden, 2007.

14. McClatchy-Tribune News Service, "Wis. Teen Pleads Guilty in Facebook Sex Case," Boulder Weekly.com, http:// www.boulderweekly.com/ article-862-wis-teen-pleads-guilty-in-facebook-sex-case. html (Posted December 22, 2009).

15. Bianca Prieto, "More Teenagers See Serious Consequences of 'Sexting' Nude Pics," *Orlando Sentinel,* http:// www.pantagraph.com/news/ article_47elb9c5-7741-59c6-98b0-d263745509ef.html (Posted March 11 2009).

CHAPTER 5

1. The Serial Killer Database, "John Robinson," The Serial Killer Database http:// www.serialkillerdatabase.net/ johnrobinson.html (Accessed August 4, 2009).

2. Mark Gribben, "Cruel Intentions," *Trutv.com,* http:// www.trutv.com/library/crime/ serial_killers/predators/john_ robinson/index.html (Accessed August 30, 2009).

3. James McLaughlin, "Cyber Child Sex Offender Typology," http://www.ci.keen.nh.us/ police/typology.html (Accessed September 1, 2009).

4. Kimberly Young, "Profiling Online Sex Offenders, Cyber-Predators, and Pedophiles,"

Journal of Behavioral Profiling 5, no. 1 (December 2004): 7.

5. Young, 2004.

6. Young, 2004.

7. Sean Elder, "Former Disney Exec Dodges a Bullet," *Salon. com,* http://www.salon.com/ media/col/elde/1999/12/22/ naughtonwalks/ (Posted December 22, 1999).

8. Young, 2005.

9. David Finkelhor and Kimberly Mitchell, "Internet-initiated Sex Crimes Against Minors: Implications for Prevention Based on Findings from a National Study," *Journal of Adolescent Health* 35, no. 5 (November 2004): 11–20.

10. Finkelhor and Mitchell, 2004.

11. Finkelhor and Mitchell, 2004.

12. Joan Arehart-Treichel, "Pedophilia Often in Headlines, But Not in Research Labs," *Psychiatric News* 41, no. 10 (May 19, 2006): 37.

13. Jen Stadler, "Online Child Molesters," *Netsmartz.org,* http://www.netsmartz.org/ news/onlinemolesters.htm (Posted November 14, 2009).

14. Keith Epps, "Man Receives 86 Years in Prison in Internet Sex Case: Jury Recommends 86 Years for Internet Predator," *McClatchy-Tribune Business News,* July 15, 2008.

15. Gary Grado, "Man Arrested in Rape Shown Live on Internet," *McClatchy-Tribune Business News,* June 3, 2009.

16. Mark Spencer, "Police Say BU Student, Charged in Craigslist

Killing, Robbed Women to Pay Debts," *McClatchy-Tribune Business News,* April 22, 2009.

CHAPTER 6

1. Lynn Burke, "Memoir of a Pedophile's Victim," Wired. com, http://www.wired. com/print/culture/lifestyle/ news/2000/04/35843 (Accessed August 10, 2009).

2. Thedailyreview.com, "E-Stop Law Purges NY Sex Offenders from Facebook and MySpace," Thedailyreview.com, http:// thedailyreview.com/news/e-stop-law-purges-ny-sex-offenders-from-facebook-and-myspace-1.457378?localLin ksEnabled=false (Accessed December 5, 2009).

3. Kathleen Foody, "Man Caught in Online Sex Sting," *McClatchy-Tribune Business News,* July 22, 2009.

4. PR Newswire, "National Cyber-Tipline Tops 500,000 Reports," http://www.prnewswire.com/ news-releases/national-cybertipline-tops-500000-reports-52719712.html/ (Accessed January 1, 2010).

5. Janis Wolak, David Finkelhor, and Kimberly Mitchell, "Trends in Arrests of 'Online Predators,'" *Crimes Against Children Research Center,* http://www.unh.edu/ccrc/pdf/ CV194.pdf (Accessed June 25, 2010).

6. Wolak, Finkelhor, and Mitchell, "Trends."

7. Wolak, Finkelhor, and Mitchell, "Trends."

8. Wolak, Finkelhor, and Mitchell, "Trends."

9. Wolak, Finkelhor, and Mitchell, "Trends."

10. Wolak, Finkelhor, and Mitchell, "Trends."

11. Wolak, Finkelhor, and Mitchell, "Trends."

12. Todd Richmond, "More Internet Predators are Challenging Agents," *Chicago Tribune,* March 21, 2009.

13. Richmond, 2009.

14. Michael Kozak, "Child Pornography," *Encyclopedia of Cybercrime* (Santa Barbara, Calif.: Greenwood Press, 2009), 24.

15. Wendy Walsh and Janis Wolak, "Nonforcible Internet-Related Sex Crimes with Adolescent Victims: Prosecution Issues and Outcomes," *Child Maltreatment* 10, no. 3 (August 2005): 260.

16. Walsh and Wolak, 2005.

17. Microsoft News Center, "New Technology Fights Child Porn by Tracking Its 'PhotoDNA,'" Microsoft. com, http://www.microsoft. com/presspass/features/ 2009/dec09/12-15PhotoDNA. mspx (Accessed January 2, 2010).

CHAPTER 7

1. Melissa Wells and Kimberly J. Mitchell, "How do High-Risk Youth Use the Internet? Characteristics and

Implications for Prevention," *Child Maltreatment* 13, no. 3 (March 18, 2008): 1.

2. The Associated Press, "Feds Arrest 50 in Bust of Child Porn Ring," CBS.com, http://www.cbsnews.com/stories/2010/05/26/national/main6521695.shtml (Posted May 26, 2010).

Arehart-Treichel, J. "Pedophilia Often in Headlines, But Not in Research Labs." *Psychiatric News* 41, no. 10 (May 19, 2006): 37.

Associated Press. "Teen Runs up Dad's Cell Bill to Nearly $22,000." MSNBC.com. Available online. URL: http://www.msnbc.msn.com/id/34445748/ns/technology_and_science-tech_and_gadgets/ Accessed January 23, 2009.

Burke, Lynn. "Memoir of a Pedophile's Victim." *Wired.* Available online. URL: http://www.wired.com/print/culture/lifestyle/news/2000/04/35843 Accessed August 10, 2009.

CBS News. "An Online Tragedy," CBSNews.com. Available online. URL: http://www.cbsnews.com/stories/2000/03/23/48hours/main175556.shtml Accessed August 10, 2009.

CBS News. "Craigslist Killer Gets Life Without Parole." CBSNews.com. Available online. URL: http://www.cbsnews.com/stories/2009/04/01/national/main4911771.shtml Accessed January 1, 2010.

Chodak, Adam. "Dad Hammers Wyo. Teen's Phone after Mega-Bill." *Denverpost.com.* Available online. URL: http://www.denver-post.com/breakingnews/ci_12097656 Posted April 8, 2009.

Cockerell, Penny. "Cyber Predators Target Children." *Knight Ridder. Tribune Business News,* May 21, 2006.

Thedailyreview.com. "E-Stop Law Purges NY Sex Offenders from Facebook and MySpace." Thedailyreview.com. Available online. URL: http://thedailyreview.com/news/e-stop-law-purges-ny-sex-offenders-from-facebook-and-myspace-1.457378?localLinks Enabled=false Accessed December 5, 2009.

Elder, Sean. "Former Disney Exec Dodges a Bullet." *Salon.com.* Available online. URL: http://www.salon.com/media/col/elde/1999/12/22/naughtonwalks/ Posted on December 22, 1999.

Epps, Keith. "Man Receives 86 Years in Prison in Internet Sex Case: Jury Recommends 86 Years for Internet Predator." *McClatchy-Tribune Business News,* July 15, 2008.

Finkelhor, David, and Kimberly Mitchell. "Internet-initiated Sex Crimes Against Minors: Implications for Prevention Based on Findings from a National Study." *Journal of Adolescent Health* 35, no. 5 (November 2004): 11–20.

Foody, Kathleen. "Man Caught in Online Sex Sting." *McClatchy-Tribune Business News,* July 22, 2009.

Grado, Gary. "Man Arrested in Rape Shown Live on Internet." *McClatchy-Tribune Business News,* June 3, 2009.

Gribben, Mark. "Cruel Intentions." *Trutv.com.* Available online. URL: http://www.trutv.com/library/crime/serial_killers/predators/john_robinson/index.html Accessed August 30, 2009.

Hardesty, Greg. "My Daughter Racked up 14,528 Text Messages in One Month." *Orange County Register.com.* Available online. URL: http://www.ocregister.com/news/text-185518-phone-texting.html?pic=6 Posted January 7, 2009.

Hempel, Jessi. "Protecting Your Kids From Cyber-Predators." *Business Week*, December 12, 2005.

Hewitt, Bill, Siobhan Morrissey, and Pam Grout. "Did Cruel Hoax Lead to Suicide?" *People,* December 3, 2007, 135–136.

Hinkelman, Michael. "Perv Gets 13 1/2 Years for Yearlong Abuse of 10-Year-Old Girl." *McClatchy Business News*, July 15, 2008.

Katiesplace.org. "Christina's Story." Available online. URL: http://www.katiesplace.org/christina/christinas_story.html Accessed August 30, 2009.

Kozak, Michael, and Samuel C. McQuade (ed.). "Child Pornography." *Encyclopedia of Cybercrime*. Santa Barbara, Calif.: Greenwood Press, 2009.

Lepkowski, Paul, and Samuel C. McQuade (ed.). "Denial of Service Attacks." *Encyclopedia of Cybercrime*. Santa Barbara, Calif.: Greenwood Press, 2009.

Lenhart, Amanda. "Cyber Bullying and Online Teens." *Data Memo from Pew Internet & American Life Project*, (2007): 1.

Lenhart, Amanda, Mary Madden, Alexandra Macgill, and Aaron Smith. "Teens and Social Media." *Pew Internet & American Life Project*. Available online. URL: http://www.pewinternet.org/Reports/2007/Teens-and-Social-Media.aspx Posted December 19, 2007.

Lenhart, Amanda, Mary Madden, and Paul Hitlin. "Teens and Technology." *Pew Internet & American Life Project*. Available online. URL: http://www.pewinternet.org/Reports/2005/Teens-and-Technology.aspx Posted July 27, 2005.

Lenhart, Amanda, and Mary Madden. "Teens, Privacy, and Online Social Networks." *Pew Internet & American Life Project*. Available online. URL: http://www.pewinternet.org/Reports/2007/Teens-Privacy-and-Online-Social-Networks.aspx Posted April 18, 2007.

Loftus, Christine. "Teen Murdered by Man She Met in Chatroom." *Netsmartz.org*. Available online. URL: http://www.netsmartz.org/news/Dec02-02.htm/ Posted on December 2, 2002.

McClatchy-Tribune News Service. "Wis. Teen Pleads Guilty in Facebook Sex Case." *Boulder Weekly*. Available online. URL: http://www.boulderweekly.com/article-862-wis-teen-pleads-guilty-in-facebook-sex-case.html Accessed January 15, 2009.

McLaughlin, James. "Cyber Child Sex Offender Typology." Available online. URL: http://www.ci.keen.nh.us/police/typology.html Accessed August 30, 2009.

McQuade, Samuel C. *RIT Survey of Internet and At-Risk Behaviors*. Rochester, N.Y.: Rochester Institute of Technology, 2008.

———. "Fraudulent Schemes and Theft Online." *Encyclopedia of Cybercrime.* Santa Barbara, Calif.: Greenwood Press, 2009.

———, James P. Colt, and Nancy B.B. Meyers. *CyberBullying: Protecting Kids & Adults from Online Bullies.* Santa Barbara, Calif.: Praeger, 2009.

Microsoft News Center, "New Technology Fights Child Porn by Tracking Its 'PhotoDNA." Available online. URL: http://www.microsoft.com/presspass/features/2009/dec09/12-15PhotoDNA.mspx   Posted December 15, 2009.

Mills, Elinor. "DoS Attack on Twitter Targeted Specific User." *Cbs2.com.* Available online. URL: http://cbs2.com/business/social.media.attack.2.1119244.html Posted August 7, 2009.

Neal, Rome. "Internet Murder: Tips Every Parent Should Know." *Cbsnews.com.* Available online. URL: http://www.cbsnews.com/stories/2003/05/07/earlyshow/living/parenting/main552841.shtml Posted on May 8, 2003.

Prieto, Bianca. "More Teenagers See Serious Consequences of 'Sexting' Nude Pics." *Orlando Sentinel.* Available online. URL: http://www.pantagraph.com/news/article_47elb9c5-7741-59c6-98b0-d263745509ef.html Posted March 11 2009.

PR Newswire. "National CyberTipline Tops 500,000 Reports," Available online. URL: http://www.prnewswire.com/news-releases/national-cybertipline-tops-500000-reports-527/ Accessed January 1, 2010.

Richmond, Todd. "More Internet Predators are Challenging Agents." *Chicago Tribune.* March 21, 2009.

The Serial Killer Database. "John Robinson." Available online. URL: http://www.serialkillerdatabase.net/johnrobinson.html Accessed August 4, 2009.

Spencer, Mark. "Police Say BU Student, Charged in Craigslist Killing, Robbed Women to Pay Debts." *McClatchy-Tribune Business News.* April 22, 2009.

Stadler, Jen. "Online Child Molesters." *Netsmartz.org.* Available online. URL: http://www.netsmartz.org/news/onlinemolesters. htm Posted November 14, 2009.

Suler, John. "The Online Disinhibition Effect." *CyberPsychology and Behavior* 7, no. 3 (July 28, 2004): 321–326.

Walsh, Wendy, and Janis Wolak. "Nonforcible Internet-Related Sex Crimes with Adolescent Victims: Prosecution Issues and Outcomes." *Child Maltreatment* 10, no. 3 (August 2005): 260.

Wells, Melissa, and Kimberly Mitchell. "How do High-Risk Youth Use the Internet? Characteristics and Implications for Prevention." *Child Maltreatment* 13, no. 3 (March 18, 2008): 1.

Willard, Nancy. *Cyberbullying and Cyberthreats: Responding to the Challenge of Online Social Cruelty, Threats, and Distress.* Eugene, OR: Center for Safe and Responsible Internet Use, 2006.

Wolak, Janis, Kimberly Mitchell, and David Finkelhor. "Online Victimization of Youth: Five Years Later." *National Center for Missing and Exploited Children.* Available online. URL: http:// www.missingkids.com/en_US/publications/NC167.pdf Accessed June 25, 2010.

Wolak, Janis, David Finkelhor, and Kimberly Mitchell. "Trends in Arrests of 'Online Predators.'" *Crimes Against Children Research Center.* Available online. URL: http://www.unh.edu/ccrc/pdf/ CV194.pdf Accessed June 25, 2010.

Young, Kimberly. "Profiling Online Sex Offenders, Cyber-Predators, and Pedophiles." *Journal of Behavioral Profiling* 5, no. 1 (December 2004): 7.

Yurgelun-Todd, Deborah. "Inside the Teenage Brain." *PBS.org.* April 5, 2008. Available online. URL: http://www.pbs.org/wgbh/ pages/frontline/shows/teenbrain/interviews/ Posted April 5, 2008.

● ● ● FURTHER RESOURCES ● ● ●

BOOKS

Jenkins, Phillip. *Beyond Tolerance: Child Pornography on the Internet.* New York: New York University Press, 2003.

Salter, Anna. *Predators: Pedophiles, Rapists, and Other Sex Offenders.* New York: Basic Books, 2004.

Sommers, Michael. *The Dangers of Online Predators.* New York: Rosen Central, 2008.

ARTICLES

Wolak, Janis, David Finkelhor, Kimberly Mitchell, and Michael Ybarra. "Online Predators and Their Victims: Myths, Realities, and Implications for Prevention and Treatment." *American Psychologist* 63, no. 2 (March 2008): 111–128.

Ybarra, Michael and Kimberly Mitchell. "How Risky are Social Networking Sites? A Comparison of Places Online Where Youth Sexual Solicitation and Harassment Occurs." *Pediatrics* 121 (January 2008): 350–357.

WEB SITES

Crimes Against Children Research Center
http://www.unh.edu/ccrc

Cyber Safety and Ethics Initiative
http://www.rrcsei.org

iKeepSafe.org
http://ikeepsafe.org

National Center for Missing and Exploited Children
http://www.missingkids.com

●●● INDEX ●●●

Page numbers in *italics* indicate photos or illustrations.

● ● ● ABOUT THE AUTHOR ● ● ●

DR. JAMES P. COLT is the Coordinator of School Safety and Security for the Monroe 1 BOCES (Board of Cooperative Educational Services). He is a former police officer employed by the State University of New York, and also served as a criminal justice instructor and school community safety specialist at Monroe 1 BOCES. He is also a certified public school teacher, and school administrator in New York State. He earned a masters degree in criminal justice from Buffalo State College, and also holds a masters degree in educational administration from St. John Fisher College. He also earned his doctorate from St. John Fisher College, with a research focus on cyberbullying and cyberoffending. He is the co-author of *Cyber Bullying: Protecting Kids and Adults from Online Bullies* (Praeger Publishers, 2009) and contributing author to *Encyclopedia of CyberCrime* (Greenwood Press, 2009). He also serves on the executive committee of the Cyber Safety and Ethics Initiative in western New York. He is a frequent presenter at conferences and workshops on topics related to cyber-safety, bullying, violence prevention and crisis intervention, and emergency preparedness.

ABOUT THE
● ● ● CONSULTING EDITOR ● ● ●

MARCUS K. ROGERS, Ph.D., CISSP, DFCP, is the director of the Cyber Forensics Program in the department of computer and information technology at Purdue University, a former police officer, and the editor in chief of the *Journal of Digital Forensic Practice*. He has written, edited, and reviewed numerous articles and books on cybercrime. He is a professor, university faculty scholar, and research faculty member at the Center for Education and Research in Information Assurance and Security. He is also the international chair of the Law, Compliance and Investigation Domain of the Common Body of Knowledge (CBK) committee, chair of the Ethics Committee for the Digital and Multimedia Sciences section of the American Academy of Forensic Sciences, and chair of the Certification and Test Committee—Digital Forensics Certification Board. As a police officer he worked in the area of fraud and computer crime investigations. Dr. Rogers sits on the editorial board for several professional journals. He is also a member of various national and international committees focusing on digital forensic science and digital evidence. Dr. Rogers is the author of books, book chapters, and journal publications in the field of digital forensics and applied psychological analysis. His research interests include applied cyber-forensics, psychological digital crime scene analysis, cybercrime scene analysis, and cyber-terrorism. He is a frequent speaker at international and national information assurance and security conferences, and guest lectures throughout the world.